THE INTERNET:
ARE CHILDREN IN CHARGE?

Theory of Digital Supervision

CHARLENE E. DOAK-GEBAUER

B.Ed., Hon. Bus. Specialist, Special Education,
Computer Science, Network Administration,
Registered Holistic Nutritionist

The Internet: Are children in charge?
Copyright © 2019 by Charlene E. Doak-Gebauer

Tellwell Talent
www.tellwell.ca

ISBN
978-0-2288-2225-7 (Hardcover)
978-0-2288-2224-0 (Paperback)
978-0-2288-2326-1 (eBook)

TABLE OF CONTENTS

FOREWORD

It gives me great pleasure to present this book by Charlene Doak-Gebauer. Charlene has devoted close to a Decade in pursuit of Justice for Children.

In this book, she has stared down the devil and named it: Child Exploitation. Drawing on her own experience, and the experiences of many others, she cogently presents the horrible problem, and suggests some excellent solutions. Readers will be amazed at just how pervasive this problem is, and how it has infected all levels of society.

No longer can we stand by and allow children to be exploited in such a terrible fashion! Don't just read the book, BE PART OF THE SOLUTION!!

Dr. Gary R. Munn, M.Ed, PhD.

ENDORSEMENTS

This book is a wake-up call for parents, teachers, health professionals and policy makers. It underscores the degree to which, as a society, we have abandoned our young to navigate the perils of the internet on their own. We are given a chilling account of how easily children are exploited by sexual predators and often victimized by their own naivete. Charlene challenges us all to become more digitally literate and pro-actively vigilant in protecting the youngest and most vulnerable among us. At the same time, she provides a timely and invaluable resource for all responsible child care givers.

ROSE A. DYSON ED.D.
Consultant in Media Education
Author:
MIND ABUSE Media Violence in an Information Age

For years, we have had to teach our children about "street smarts". They needed to know stranger danger, be careful in parks and malls, choose your friends well, and so many safety issues.

Now, we should be teaching them computer smarts, based on the same street-smart principals we continue to use. It is too easy for individuals of the opposite sex to pose as loving and caring people. But, before they know it, young teen aged girls and boys can easily be lured into a trap that may lead ultimately, to exploitation and unhealthy sexual activity. Our young girls and boys require guidance from an adult who can help them make appropriate choices so they can mature with self-esteem and confidence.

Charlene has researched and written her Theory of Digital Supervision to help parents and adult allies supervise children. We cannot put the ownership of appropriate choices online on our children. They require guidance from adults. Toward this end, Digital Supervision provides the information for parents to be able to supervise and provide guidance online.

The approach in this book has been realistic, from providing a play to illustrate the innocence of children online, to interviewing people with real-life experiences that illustrate the magnitude of the challenges children and families face in this digital world. This is a must read for all parents, grandparents, adult allies, and professionals.

ALISON PEARCE, B.A., B.ED., M.ED., L.R.A.M
Educator and Author
Teacher, Special Education Consultant, Principal, Trustee
Toronto, Ontario

DEDICATION

This book is dedicated to:

My family, particularly little "M";

All of the precious children in the world; may they be protected against online dangers.

The survivors of the horrendous crime of Internet Child Exploitation. This crime permeates our existence, from child pornography, to sex trafficking, to child abductions, to cyberbullying, to sex slavery, to suicide, and more.

INTRODUCTION

Welcome to my second book on my Theory of Digital Supervision. Included at the end of this book, is my personal history, as was included in my first book. I believe it is important that readers know and understand the history of the development of Digital Supervision.

Thank you for caring enough to read this book, and trying to make a difference for your children and families, and globally. Practice and application of Digital Supervision will help to develop safer online environments for the proactive protection of children and families.

This edition is more comprehensive, with real-life interviews including: criminal lawyer (who has defended predators), police officer, psychotherapist, child pornography victim/survivor, wife of a child pornography victim/survivor, and a victim/survivor of parental sexual abuse. Information from these interviews can help readers understand the seriousness of crimes which are affecting children.

My experiences as an educator, Computer Specialist in Education, and Network Administrator, have fostered the creation of Digital Supervision. It is written in user-friendly language so that all should be able to understand. A proactive approach is preferred for online child protection.

Digital Supervision is defined as a new branch of traditional parenting that includes digital guidance and supervision of children and youth. This generation is far too independent from parental guidance and supervision. We need to catch up to the digital age.

We cannot depend on Facebook, social media, Internet Service Providers, the government, and other platforms to protect our children. Parents are ultimately responsible for the safety of their children. Digital Supervision will give adults the confidence and ability to engage in online proactive child protection. We have to take back our children and avoid having the Internet "bring them up", consume, and leave them open to predation and other vulnerabilities.

CHAPTER 1

ARE CHILDREN IN CHARGE?

The Internet: Are children in charge? **Yes, they are.**

If you have said or heard other people say, "My kids know more than I do. I don't know what they are doing on their devices", I guarantee your children are in charge of the Internet in your home. No need to feel lonely about it. I have presented globally and I hear the same complaint in every country. Parents and professionals are desperate to have a solution.

It is time to change our parenting and supervision skills to catch up to the digital age. In that most parents are in the same situation; no fingers are being pointed. Digital parenting is now necessary. We can no longer parent using just the traditional methods of parenting. Traditional must be combined with digital.

As a Computer Specialist and Network Administrator in education, I have been challenged with many situations involving students, colleagues, and parents. In addition, my family was affected by the crime of child pornography. A family member was targeted by predators at the age of four. As a Network Administrator, I had to deal with the same type of crime through finding child pornography on a computer I was reimaging. You don't understand the magnitude of the horrific assault on children unless you have the misfortune of being a victim either directly, or a victim by proxy (viewing of child sexual exploitation pictures causing trauma). My family has been victimized two times, two separate cities, two different members, too many times.

As a result of the traumas in my family, all members were affected, from the parents, to grandparents, to siblings, to cousins, and more. I wondered how I could change things. The depression and negative feelings brought many of us to despair. I decided I would use my expertise in computers and experience as an educator to develop a theory for supervising children on digital devices that would be user friendly for the average person. I wanted to change such a negative into a positive for my family and all children.

It is called "Theory of Digital Supervision". The term "Digital Supervision" has registered copyright. How do we supervise our children digitally? It is necessary in this digital age.

Parents, grandparents, and adult allies need to learn more about the history of the Internet. Such knowledge will provide emphasis regarding the "speed" with which the Internet has progressed, and how much we are behind in our understanding of Internet predation and the vulnerability of our children and families.

The Internet was becoming more common in the year 2000. Schools were beginning to enable access to the Internet through their networks.

I was a teacher and Network Administrator, managing a new network in a school. To emphasize the progress of the Internet in the year 2000, we were amazed at a moving picture on the screen – the animated gif. This has progressed to live streaming for everything from movies to Facebook live, which illustrates the magnitude and speed of change. The adjustment to parenting with the Internet and the use of digital devices is difficult.

The Theory of Digital Supervision is divided into three parts:

Awareness – it is important to know and comprehend the reality of the challenges we face every time a child is on a computer, gaming device, cellphone, and other devices. Unfortunately, too many parents believe having a child is much easier with the Internet. Any screen in front of a child poses increased challenges for child protection. Predators know where to go to find the greatest number of prey – the Internet.

The greatest component of awareness: when a gateway to the Internet is provided in a home, parental responsibility needs to be understood as being much greater. The activity of children and teens on digital devices should be monitored. So often, it is not. Throughout this book, the awareness segment of Digital Supervision will be emphasized.

Method – how to supervise children and families digitally. Digital Supervision includes the use of a computer filter. Digital Supervision should be considered as being "interdependent" with a filter. What is a filter? This will be explained later.

Hope – As adults, we WILL be able to supervise our children through Digital Supervision, and we must.

Awareness is the most challenging. Too many people are in denial. When I present internationally, or within my country, I have been taken aside by members of the audience and told "this is a problem in our country. You have to speak to a larger audience and make a bigger difference. You need to be here and present to all parents." To readers, based on research and experience, this is a global problem and one that has to be dealt with through Digital Supervision.

Our children are being exposed to more violence, pornography, sadism, bullying, suicide, and other negative issues, than any generation in the history of the world. We need to catch up in order to guide this generation realistically. We can do this and need to do so.

Most people are using the Internet in some form on a daily basis, be it through computer, laptop, iPad, cellphone, gaming, or other device. Too often, digital device users believe their activities are benign to any type of interference based on their security settings on their devices and in various environments (software, social media, websites, and the like).

The content of this book will illustrate to readers how vulnerable they are on the Internet, and the necessary precautions they need to take to be protected, as well as for child and family protection.

Predators? The Internet hosts more predation than any host in the history of the world. There are multiple sources of predation – child predator, sex trafficking, domestic servitude, terrorist radicalization, forced labour, bonded labour, child labour, and forced marriage, to name a few.

Do you know of anyone who has been victimized? Of course, you do – you may not realize it. Parents often lack the realization where their children are concerned. There are victims of Internet predators in every backyard, street corner, school, professional environment, places of worship, and more.

Many children can be addicted to porn and their parents are totally unaware. Although the DSM does not list pornography as an addiction disorder, it is best to refer to this as a "porn-related addictive disorder". When this porn-related addictive disorder begins, it can escalate to higher levels of porn, to where children are stealing money from parents (through credit card use or other means) to obtain the higher levels of porn. There are methods of relieving your child of this type of addiction, however, too many times children have a porn-related addictive disorder in silence. [1]

According to ASAM (American Society of Addiction Medicine), addiction is defined as:

"A primary, chronic disease of brain reward, motivation, memory and related circuitry. This is reflected in an individual pathologically pursuing reward and/ or relief by substance use and other behaviors. It is characterized by inability to consistently abstain, impairment in behavioral control, craving, diminished recognition of significant problems with one's behaviors and interpersonal relationships, and a dysfunctional emotional response. Like other chronic diseases, addiction often involves cycles of relapse and remission. Without treatment or engagement in recovery activities, addiction is progressive and can result in disability or premature death." (ASAM, n.d.) [2]

Any addiction can be debilitating; however, a porn addiction of a child can be an insidious addiction.

The child loses their innocence. The child becomes confused, which can lead to self-damaging thoughts. Children are not prepared for, nor do they understand sex, which can be presented online in the form of pictures, or audio/video files. There is an age restriction for pornography in order to protect children (usually 18 years of age). With the Internet, this has become problematic because of the ease of access of such files, as well as, the way predators make the material accessible to our children.

Our children, too often, are being "brought up" by digital devices and the Internet; these devices segregate child from parent, to an alarming degree. Few parents supervise the devices they provide. Having time outs and removing the devices periodically, are ineffective options because the exposure can be there whenever they are online.

Globally, children and youth are putting themselves in detrimental situations in epidemic proportions. School personnel interviewed have stated they have no idea where to turn. Children and youth have "nudes", which is their reference to pictures of friends and themselves nude (legal terminology "self-exploitation"), on their devices. When the pictures are of anyone under the age of 18, it is defined as "child pornography" in most countries, which is a crime.

Child Pornography? The crime of "child pornography" has existed for many years. There are stories from ancient Greece and Rome, which have narrated the sexual abuse of children with drawings as illustrations (not considered a crime at the time). Unfortunately, child pornography was not recognized as a crime until 1977, which is incredible. And, this was prior to the digital age becoming an everyday option in homes.

In the United States, for example:

1977 – The Protection of Children Against Sexual Exploitation Act was developed. The federal law specified that for-profit production and distribution of child pornography would have legal consequences.

1984 – The Child Protection Act criminalized the activity of non-profit child pornography trafficking.

1986 – Realization that child pornography had long-lasting effects on children.

1990 – it became illegal to be in possession of child pornography.

1999 – international investigations of child pornography began.

2015 – all states had laws against distribution, and possession of child pornography, either for profit or not-for-profit. (U.S. Department of Justice).

July 23, 2002 – In Canada, the offence of accessing child pornography was added to the Canadian Criminal Code.

July 20, 2005 – In Canada, Bill C-2 was amended. Inclusion of mandatory minimum penalties; and the definition of child pornography included written and audio materials. The full Canadian Criminal Code legislation related to the crime of child pornography is in Appendix C of this book. It is provided so all readers will comprehend the definition and extent of the crime in Canada and many countries.

Many people have stated they found it horrendous that child pornography was not a crime until 1977. Such abuse and degradation of children was "legal" before that time; however, the sexual assault shown on the pictures was not. It is disgusting, to say the least.

Victimization of children using any type of abuse, is vile. The sexual assault and filming are horrific to the victim. To have such assault filmed in any way causes trauma – the Internet houses it forever. Victims often wonder who is watching their video or viewing their picture in the world.

Prior to the Internet, the pictures and videos were viewed in pedophile secret communication "rings", with an underground organization. Now, they are still viewed in pedophile secret rings, but it has become a global, more accessible "family" of twisted individuals who prey on our vulnerable children daily.

Unfortunately, the Internet has helped predators and pedophiles find each other easily. I say "predators" because not all abusers/child pornographers are categorized as "pedophiles". There are heterosexual couples using their children as part of their child pornography enterprise. This is a multi-billion-dollar industry, at all levels of society. When speaking with various police Internet Child Exploitation units, they have explained that wherever I present, there will be someone involved in the crime in any audience. This crime is everywhere.

To make this clear, the following statistics will illustrate the magnitude of the problem. The data was collected in 2007 and republished in 2018. The figures have grown exponentially since then.

20,000 children are victimized daily through sexual exploitation (taken from police oral presentation); this equals 7,300,000 annually;

116,000 daily searches for child pornography websites;

24.5 million adult porn websites;

Yearly production:

13,000 adult videos; Hollywood 507 movies;

Annual profit:

Adult porn $13 billion; Hollywood $8.8 billion;

Over 20% of adults and 80% of children are exposed to porn unintentionally. [3]

In London, Ontario, Canada, a pediatric photographer was charged with producing and distributing child pornography. The child being used was from a heterosexual couple in a nearby city. They "sold" their child as part of their income. The predator being used for the videos was transgender. Not all transgender people are pedophiles, which needs to be clear to all readers. The case, at the writing of this book, was still in the courts.

The pedophile community, within their "family" of friends, has decided they would like acceptance. They refer to themselves as "Pedsexuals" or "Pedosexuals" or "Minor Attracted Persons". They believe they should be accepted within the LGBTQ community. They even have established logos, one of which is the Greek Omega symbol, with a smaller Omega symbol inside.

No one group should be viewed as pedophiles based on sexual orientation (heterosexual, bisexual, pansexual, lesbian, homosexual, transgendered, etc.). Pedophiles are in a community all their own – a community that believes being abusive and violent toward children is "acceptable". More people in society are becoming aware of this movement.

Anyone who believes that sexual abuse of little children lacks violence, is terribly mistaken. It is a violation of emotional and physical health. Many children who have been abused, have permanent physical damage.

Child pornography is a part of the crime human trafficking. Many children from ages one month to age 18 are advertised using products identified as child pornography, and are used for the purpose of human trafficking/sex trafficking. Fighting child pornography is necessary for the protection of all children.

After interviewing victims of child pornography, it was obvious to me these victims have a life-long challenge. I have had therapists tell me that child pornography is "just" child sexual abuse. This type of abuse is far more than "just" child sexual abuse. The pictures of the victims are out there forever. The victims and their families know it. To treat this type of abuse as "just child sexual abuse", is a questionable point of view. However, opinions are changing, and victims are meeting with therapists who are understanding their daily torment – not just the abuse, but the circulation of their picture or video........forever.

Whether you are a parent, teen, child, professional ally, aunt, uncle, grandparent – we all have a duty to protect OUR children. As you read this book, you will begin to realize the extent of this digital epidemic.

My Theory of Digital Supervision© is for child and family protection, and should be used by all households and professionals. I believe it should be a household term.

We need to concentrate on

> "humanity supervising humanity,
> again, but digitally".
>
> Charlene Doak-Gebauer

Child sexual abuse material has exploded with the introduction of the Internet. It is a growing crime, and one ALL people should realize is threatening our children, families, and general public sense of decency toward children.

The scale of the problem.
2004 = 450,000 files; 2015 = 25 million files*

*The number of child sexual abuse
files reviewed by the National Center
for Missing & Exploited Children.

63% of victimized kids Thorn encountered had been advertised online. As many as one in six runaways reported to the National Center for Missing and Exploited Children (United States) likely became victims of sex trafficking."

Wearethorn.org. [4]

CHAPTER 2

SUPERVISION HISTORY

DIGITAL SUPERVISION NECESSITY

Parents, caregivers, and professionals need to "reconceptualize" their definition of child protection and supervision of children and youth. It is necessary that the old supervision methods of child protection be supplemented with, and include, "the Theory of Digital Supervision". Parenting MUST catch up to the digital age.

In previous years (before 1990), parents were able to monitor the activities of their children fairly closely. There were landlines, TV, malls, sports teams, playgrounds, parks, churches, and the like. Parents often spoke of their challenges in keeping their children safe.

With the introduction of the Internet, there has been an explosion of various challenges for parents. It has come so fast; the general population is overwhelmed with the challenges of having their children on the Internet and various digital devices.

I challenge all adults to catch up to the digital age. No longer should parents be saying "they know more than I do about these devices". No longer should parents be saying "my child is so smart, they are way ahead of me". No longer should parents be saying "I really don't know how to supervise my children digitally".

As a parent, it is the responsibility of adults to monitor the activities of children, not only to keep them safe, but to monitor their communications. Even if adults do not have children, or their children have left the "nest", we all need to know and understand Digital Supervision for the sake of the future of this generation. We are all aware of children – our own, nieces, nephews, neighbours, etc. We are all responsible for children, regardless of relationship. A grandparent or aunt or uncle? Read the following example of a possible situation and decide if you need to know about Digital Supervision.

There is always the possibility of this type of scenario: you are a grandparent or aunt/uncle. Your relative under the age of 18 comes for a visit. They are working on their cell phone and you believe everything is okay.

About one week later, the police arrive at your door. They ask you if you were responsible for your 15-year old relative on a specific date and time. You will respond with a nervous "yes". They then proceed to tell you that at the time the fifteen-year-old was visiting, they were trading "nudes" of friends from school, which is considered child pornography because the pictures were nudes of someone under the age of 18.

It then becomes your responsibility because the minor was in your care and you were the adult in charge at the time. It is not a situation people want to be in. Would charges be laid on the relative supervising? It is difficult to determine, because every situation is open to interpretation by law enforcement; however, would you want to have this conversation with law enforcement?

After interviewing grandparents and other relations, they have indicated they have very few restrictions for the use of the Wi-Fi in their homes. Children often realize this and enjoy going to relatives' homes to enable their full liberty to engage in communications that might otherwise be restricted.

It used to be that parents played board games, cards, sports, etc. with their children. Or, that children went to each other's homes to engage in activities, usually with a responsible adult in the area, that could supervise and ensure the children were communicating appropriately and they were safe.

That type of activity has been taken over with children playing online games with peers and unknowns. The cell phone generation has created mammoth "monsters" which parents have stated they have little control over and by which they feel intimidated. Furthermore, parents rarely investigate the activity of their children on digital devices, particularly cell phones.

At presentations, I ask parents if they even review the cell phone activities of their children by looking at pictures, histories, and icons on the device. The response is always – "I can't invade their privacy like that". Since when did we decide that "children" should be trained to make the right choices while on a device without parental supervision? Parental supervision is required to assist children in making appropriate choices for their age level. "Children" are incapable of making decisions without the guidance of adults, in many situations. On rare occasions, this may not be the case, however, the majority of children require guidance.

Throughout this book, the reader will be made aware of the need for the Theory of Digital Supervision; be made aware of methods of supervision; and be given hope that there is a way to supervise OUR children for the security of all of our futures.

CHAPTER 3

PARENT/CAREGIVER CONCERNS

Most parents and families are worried about abductions, playground bullying, human trafficking, sex slavery, torture, murder and anything else where children and youth are concerned. Without Digital Supervision, children and youth can be exposed to all of the above through their independent actions while surfing the Internet, chatting online, playing video games online, and other digital activities.

Parents, caregivers, and adult allies – would you give your car keys to a 12-year-old and let them drive around your city alone, unsupervised? Then, why do you give the key to your router to your children, and allow them to circulate around the world without adult guidance or supervision? Adults have to realize the extent and risk of travel over the Internet.

Parents have presented many scenarios and questions about the problems that exist with their children and families using computers and digital devices at home and elsewhere. Listed within this chapter are some common scenarios of concern. Digital Supervision skills help to circumvent these problem areas:

- Often, parents give their children a code word or phrase for the child to use to determine if a person who approaches them is a safe person. For example, a parent may say the code word is "sports". If the person picking the child up knows the code word, then the child will let the adult accompany them home or drive them in their car.

- Many children have been instructed to use the proper names for their body parts. For example, penis, breast, vagina, and others. Many parents have been instructed by professionals to do this so that children will understand the scientific names and be able to describe accurately any activity involving these body parts. This is advisable; however, parents should go a few steps further.

- Parents purchase cellphones for their children. They do this in an attempt to keep their children safe. By having a phone, a child can call their parents or caregivers to make sure the adults who care for them know their location. The cell phone could also be used to access data, if the parent or caregiver decides to purchase a data plan. Data is not always a good idea for children.
- Many homes have a computer in the open area of their home. Parents do not always monitor the activity in spite of where the computer is located.
- Too often, parents have a basic insecurity related to their knowledge in comparison to the knowledge of their children. They believe they cannot monitor because of lack of knowledge.
- Children and youth loan their phones freely to friends or unknown persons, which can cause an unsafe situation.
- Many parents share that their child has told them "other" kids take nudes of themselves and distribute them electronically to friends.
- Some children as young as five years of age are known to have been on pornography sites. Parents find this disturbing (if they are aware)

and do not understand how the children got to the sites. They require more knowledge to understand this issue and how to avoid it.

- Some spouses have found child pornography on their home computer. They realize their spouses are guilty of downloading the pictures or videos on the machine.

- Police and therapists have stated that youth and some children are addicted to viewing pornography online. Where did this come from? It could be from a predator who has shared porn or an unsolicited situation when a child has viewed pornography.

- Police have stated that children as young as eight years of age are producing, distributing, and possessing child pornography.

- Some therapists have shared that their adult clients have "accidentally" viewed child pornography.

- Youth have stated that most students or friends have nudes on their cell phones. Youth believe it to be common and that there is no problem with having these pictures on their phones. It is understood to be common that youth have pictures of themselves nude in selfies.

- Children (aged 7 to 12) have taken pictures of their genitalia and breasts using their parents' computers and mobile devices.
- Youth and children have stated that they have chatted and shared information with "unknowns".
- Youth and children have stated that they prefer the social media sites that offer texting and other communications, which claim to provide anonymity in order to omit their parents from their communications.
- Parents are afraid to invade the privacy of the activities of their children. Privacy has no boundaries when it comes to child protection.
- Parents, caregivers, and adult allies need to realize how their contributions in social media can affect their entire family.
- Adults, youth, and children often brag about the number of friends they have in social media. The differentiation between "real life friends" and "social media friends" has to be understood at all levels.
- Predation is done by sophisticated predators. They are not only in playgrounds, schools, neighbourhood gatherings, sports teams, sports events, arenas, religious buildings/

organizations, malls, stores and additional locations, they are all over the Internet. They can identify their prey through social media, gaming and other means.

- Adults, youth, and children email information to recipients who are unknowns to them. They have no idea the information they are transmitting via email.
- Parents and adult allies have stated it is difficult to instill in children an ability to refuse requests.
- Children and youth can express emotional challenges on social media for which parents should be aware.
- Children and youth can be negative communicators and require guidance to be positive with peers and online friends.

These are real concerns and need to be addressed by all parents, caregivers, and adult allies. Digital Supervision can help the detection of the following types of scenarios:

- cyberbullying (is your child a victim or a bully);
- threats of suicide;

- exposure of a child to xxx pornography – **prepare** (a child for the accidental viewing of porn); or, **repair** (the damage done by a child losing their innocence to viewing porn);
- lack of good communication skills, depression, loneliness;
- predation;
- grooming toward radicalization and violent acts to public safety.

CHAPTER 4

THEORY OF DIGITAL SUPERVISION PLAY

PLAYWRIGHT – CHARLENE DOAK-GEBAUER

This play has been performed several times before a live audience, including families, parents and children. After performances of this play, audiences have expressed enthusiasm. Parents believed viewing it with their children was of great benefit to both parent and child. They have been more alert to the issues based on a live play performance, because the dialogue of actors and situations helped to illustrate Internet safety and better choices to the audiences. A narration following each scene was given in live performances.

Please enjoy the play as you learn more about online safety through real-life scenes related to real-life situations. Following each scene is an explanation of what is happening in the scene and Digital Supervision guidelines for parents.

If you are interested in performing this play, permission must be granted by the author. Contact at <u>internetsense.first@rogers.com or phone 01-5198541249</u>.

SCENE 1 - PATTY PIG ONLINE GAME

Setting: Mother Elaine and daughter Kristal, with her friend Beth on a computer on the Internet on the right side of the stage, at Kristal's home. There is a wall between them and another unknown person on a computer on the left side of the stage (Jeremy).

The friends, Kristal and Beth, are happily playing with their mothers while they are on the computer. They are talking and laughing about everything they see on the screen. Kristal and Beth love Patty Pig and are playing an online game they found on the Internet. It is free and Kristal's Mom said it was okay to play it.

On the other side of the wall, a man enters the room. He sits down and goes on the computer.

Kristal and Beth are laughing and looking at the computer.

Elaine gets up and says: "Hey I'm going to get a coffee. You girls have fun and I will be right back. I am so glad you came over Beth."

Kristal says: "Perfect Mom. If there are any cookies, we would love to have some." The girls giggle.

Elaine: "Sure, just made some this morning lol! Oatmeal raisin, your favourite and you know it!"

Elaine walks off stage. She thinks the girls are having a great time playing online Patty Pig. Both girls love the game and are so happy and content when they are on the screen. It makes life much easier than having the girls wondering around the yard. Kristal's Mom worries every time the girls are in the yard for fear they might wander off or someone might come into the yard that they don't know.

On the other side of the wall, a man is on the computer. He concentrates on the screen. After a while, he grins and says: "Hi there. Is anyone there? I want to play Patty with you."

Kristal and Beth look at each other and are shocked.

Kristal says: "Who are you?"

Jeremy says "I am Jeremy your new friend. Hey how old are you?"

Kristal responds and says "seven years old".

On the other side of the wall, Jeremy says: "So is my son. I love playing Patty Pig with him. Do you think I could play Patty with you?" He smiles, nodding.

Kristal looks puzzled and looks at Beth. Neither girl had ever had this happen before. They are surprised. They shrug their shoulders, look at each other and nod.

Beth says "sure".

Jeremy says: "I am glad you want to. It will be fun. Where do you live? We live in Vancouver."

Beth responds with: "We live in Ingersoll." The girls giggle and look at each other.

Jeremy: "Is that in Ontario?"

Kristal: "Yes, Canada. You and your son live a long way from us don't you?"

Jeremy: "Yes we do but we could be friends at a distance. Would you like that? We want more friends and we can play Patty with you."

Kristal looks at Beth- both girls say "Yes" together and laugh with a hands up.

Beth: "We would love to be your friend. It is fun playing Patty with people online. We get bored just playing together."

Jeremy: "When is your Mom coming back?"

Kristal responds by saying "How did you know she left? I don't know – should be soon".

Jeremy: "I had a feeling your Mom left, that is all. When I play with my son's friends, parents usually leave the room after a while. Ok that's good. Parents don't always understand the game of Patty Pig. We can play and chat without any grownups. That's fun isn't it?"

Kristal and Beth shrug their shoulders, look at each other, and smile.

Kristal: "Sure, that's okay. Mom won't mind anyway. She is a cool Mom."

Jeremy nods: "Do you go to school? My son is in grade one. He is really smart."

Beth says: "Yeh, we go to school and we are really smart too!"

Jeremy nods and says: "What school do you go to? My son goes to Princess Elizabeth in Victoria, British Columbia. We are a long way away from you two I think."

Beth: "We go to Harrisfield Public School."

Jeremy smiles and says: "Do you go on the computer at school?"

Just then, the mother comes back into the room. She sits down beside the girls and asks them how they are doing. Both girls shrug their shoulders and smile.

All of a sudden, Jeremy asks again: "Hey you didn't answer yet. Do you go on the computer at school? You know, Harrisfield?"

Kristal's Mom looks at the computer, looks at the girls and Beth, and asks "Who is he? How long have you been chatting?"

Both shrug their shoulders; lift their hands and Kristal says "We don't know. A few minutes. He is a really nice man and has been chatting with us."

Beth: "Yah, he has a son in grade one like us! Nice man!."

Kristal's Mom starts asking questions "Who are you and why are you talking to my daughter and her friend? You are too old to be her friend. Get off the computer girls. We need to have a talk."

It becomes obvious that the mother is getting more concerned. She wants to know what the girls have shared, and asks who was on the chat? Is their mother or father with them? No answer.

Jeremy logs out of the chat and the Patty game immediately. Mother and girls leave the room and walk off stage.

• •

This type of situation is all too common in today's society. However, what is not common, is parents actually finding out their children are chatting with an adult during their online gaming time.

Reviewing this scene and the dialogue, the predator, Jeremy, has already begun to "groom" the children. Grooming is the process of building an emotional connection with a child to gain their trust. The goal of the predator is trust as the first step to reaching the goal of sexual abuse, sexual exploitation, abduction, or trafficking. This can be done online, face-to-face, by a stranger or by someone known. A predator could be anyone – family member, parent, older sibling or relative, adult, professional, teacher - again, anyone.

Online predator grooming has become so common with the introduction of online gaming, social media, and other vehicles for communication via the Internet.

The stages of grooming should be realized before any parent is able to educate their child about the safest defense mechanisms while online. Predators used to (and some still do) go to malls, parks, playgrounds, schools, and other public places to find their "prey". The predator is more sophisticated now, and tries to find their victims where most children are – online. And, they are becoming very good at finding them, and victimizing them.

What could be a goal for a predator?

- Asking a child to send nude photos/videos to the predator;
- talking to a child about inappropriate topics and taping it;
- sextortion (obtaining pictures and asking for more pictures to be able to sell);
- webcam sextortion – asking for nudes; asking for the victim to engage in sexual behaviour such as masturbation or personal touching; requesting the creation of different types of videos alone or with others;
- to name a few.

The first stage of grooming is finding the victim. Predators know that children are playing online games frequently. They are also aware that parents rarely know what their children are doing online. This situation makes the first stage of grooming relatively easy. The innocence of children makes them easy targets for any type of conversation online.

This scene in the play is a good example of how a predator will find a child online. He opened the conversation by saying hello. He asked how old the girls were. He then proceeded to tell them he had a son that is close to their ages. This is a part of grooming – gain the trust of the children by letting them know they have something in common. What did these children do? What most children innocently do, they talked to the "adult" and shared information that the predator would use to gain even more information.

For example, he knew how old they were and then proceeded to talk about his son and the school he attends. This opened the door for discussion about the school the girls attend. He also told them where he "lives"; the girls responded thinking it would be a benign piece of conversation because the predator told them he lived in British Columbia, a province in Canada far west of the province of Ontario where the girls live.

However, this predator could be a neighbour of the girls or even live close to the school they said they attend. This is a short scenario. It did not take long for the children to share too much information with a predator.

The next stage of grooming is gaining access to the potential victim. This predator has access to the victims, through an online gaming chat. This chat can proceed to an extent that the predator has control of the thoughts of the child. If the child trusts the predator enough, and is a lonely child, the predator can begin to groom the child through emphasizing they should not trust people in their family, only the predator; they should not trust friends, only the predator.

In the case of the scene from the play, the computer that was used was in the home of the hosting child, and contains what is known as the IP address of the computer. This is identifiable information for the predator to continually try to seek out the child and have them continue to chat and gain more trust.

The predator can actually take over the reasoning powers of the victim and control their relationships further. They will work on the child so the family might trust the intentions of the predator. The child may talk about the predator as a "good" friend, without the parents or guardians realizing the age and inappropriateness of the relationship.

Parents need to realize that not only is the child groomed, the whole family is groomed. In the case of an online predator, they will groom the child to trust their judgement with online communications with them; to obtain head phones so that their chats will be more secretive; teach them about private chat rooms on sites that might have pornographic content, and more.

The ultimate goal of the groomer is to gain trust and have the victim do things for them. In some cases, a face-to-face meeting is the goal. This would be one of the worst-case scenarios. This type of predator could want to engage in sexual assault, sexual slavery, or human trafficking. A number of victims can fall into this type of category.

Another type of online grooming victim, would be one who has had "nudes" requested. Nudes would be pictures sent by the victim to the predator online. Unfortunately, this type of predator will have the picture and can use it against the victim to request even more pictures or special types of behaviour. They will use the pictures as black mail and tell the victim they will circulate the pictures to all of the victim's friends, parents, etc. Sending nudes is an extremely dangerous situation.

There are cases known internationally where this type of victimization has occurred. Amanda Todd, in Canada, was victimized in such a way. The predator was in Europe, asked for nudes, and when they were received, he requested even more, and engaged in this type of "blackmail" with her. This can be devastating, and in the case of Amanda, the poor girl committed suicide.

Blackmail can be the result, which is the term more familiar to many people. However, this type of behaviour is now referred to as 'sextortion'. A definition of sextortion in this case is "Sextortion also refers to a form of blackmail in which sexual information or images are used to extort sexual favors from the victim. Social media and text messages are often the source of the sexual material and the threatened means of sharing it with others." (Wikipedia.org). [5] "Sextortionists" can be successful because teens rarely share the humiliating experience with anyone.

During the grooming process, the predator will work on granting romantic thoughts, gaining sexual information (or giving it).

They work on trust and keeping things a "secret".

There is a manipulation process where the predator will listen and tell them that they listen better than anyone else and care more than anyone else.

They will support the child in any way they can to make them feel that what they believe is okay.

They may share pornography with the child so that the child will view it as okay and possibly send pictures to the predator. The predator can gradually go to child pornography and attempt to educate the child into thinking what is in the child pornography pictures is "okay" thereby gaining the trust of the child so that they will engage in the same type of activity.

This type of exercise has always been done. I have interviewed multiple child pornography victims who were victimized before the age of the Internet. They were shown pornographic magazines or pictures.

The pictures were always described as "Polaroid pictures". The Polaroid picture was produced automatically using an instamatic camera. These cameras processed the film and printed the picture instantly, so that the predator did not have to go to a film processing facility. The predator then worked on convincing the victim to engage in a sexual act. The pictures would be a source of grooming and saying it is okay because the people in the pictures have done it. This is done online now but the grooming technique is the same.

Children are naturally curious and a predator accesses the victim's learning desires for the benefit of the grooming process.

Ultimately, the groomer gains trust, has the child doing things online, and then works on alienating the child from their families.

Our children can be taken over through online communications out of trust, fear, manipulation, and intimidation.

What to do? It is important that parents be actively involved with the activities of their children as they game, use social media, and other communications online. Please do not think that innocent, children's games are the answer.

Predators know some parents want to have their children on nonviolent games they believe are safe and therefore, safe for the children to play independently without supervision. The predator loves to go to the games that indicate a child is protected more than most. Reason? Such a child is usually alone, protected, and naïve. This is the type of child a predator can target.

They are good at finding their "victims" online. The digital predator is far more sophisticated than a traditional predator you might find in a park, mall, etc. And, there are so many children from which to choose. Gaming systems provide another location for their prey. Never think a child is benign to predation on specific games. Predators know where to find a child that will chat with them, on any game.

If you have two systems, play online when your children are engaged. Do it anonymously. You will not only discover their online behaviours, you may also be able to direct them for better communication skills if you discover they are a possible cyber bully, or a victim.

After teaching school, I have found it is usually the parents who are the last to know their child is a terror with other children, or online. Digital Supervision would change this lack of knowledge of the communications of children. However, I am sure there will still be parents in denial that their child is doing anything wrong.

We need to play digitally now, in addition to any other non-online activity. Playing online with your children will open more communications within your family, and uncover possible situations.

It is important to have open communication with your children daily about their online activities.

SCENE TWO – SELFIE ADDICTIONS

Setting: Three friends Nancy, Rhonda and Steve on the right side of the stage. They are discussing what they do on their devices. On the other side of the stage, is one boy, Nathan, sitting alone at the computer.

Rhonda "I love taking selfies but I just have to make the perfect one." She takes another selfie.

Nancy keeps laughing and says "I never do them – it seems so stupid."

Steve just looks at the girls and says, "selfies are a waste of time. Only people who love themselves do selfies. What do you say we play Roblox again?"

They go to the computer and sit around the screen together. They want to play Roblox and finally get online. While they are on the game, Rhonda does another selfie. Nancy and Steve look at her and roll their eyes. They both think she needs to stop doing it.

Steve says "You are obsessed with selfies and be careful who you share your picture with – people could use your pictures to do terrible things."

They start playing Roblox and realize one of their friends is playing too. They get really enthusiastic about the game.

All of a sudden, a new player comes on and asks "How are you doing?"

All three look at each other and realize they may not know the new player.

Rhonda asks "Hey!!! Who are you?"

Nathan "a friend".

They all look at each other and are getting suspicious.

Steve "What is your name?"

Nathan "Nathan".

Nancy asks "where are you from?"

Nathan "Yah, Woodstock. What high school do you all go to?".

Steve "IDCI in Ingersoll".

Nathan "I go to CASS in Woodstock".

They were all suspicious of him because none of them know a "Nathan".

Nathan "Hey Rhonda send me your picture. You are so beautiful I would like to have one to see when you're not online"

It was almost as though he had heard their conversation about selfies. All three look at each other with confusion. They wondered how he knew her name. They mumble quietly.

Rhonda "You know my name? He must have heard us talking." She looks at Steve and Nancy and shakes her head.

Nancy "Hey man you are a creep. Why would you want her picture anyway? Rhonda, don't send one."

Steve looks at Rhonda, shakes his head, and says "No – don't do it."

Nathan said, "Don't worry. I won't do anything with it. I just want to know if I know you or not."

All of a sudden, a video comes up on the screen. It was of them earlier, talking about selfies and taking the pictures. Nancy, Rhonda and Steve look at the video and are totally shocked.

Steve yells and asks "How did you get the video of us?"

Nancy "You are a creep! You have no right to take a video without our permission!"

There is no response. Then, another comes on the screen of a video Rhonda talking to her mother earlier in the day. Her laptop is in her bedroom.

Rhonda "Hey that's a video of me and my mother in my bedroom. What else could he have recorded!! I knew I shouldn't have my laptop in my room."

Steve "Dude, how did you tape our conversations? This is really weird and making us angry. Stop!"

Nancy "Yeh, stop it. How did you do that?"

All three friends stand up and start talking about the videos and Jeremy. They know they do not know the guy. They can't believe someone has recorded them talking in Rhonda's bedroom. They don't know what to do about it.

They look down at the computer again.

Steve "Holy cow, he taped us talking about selfies and has broadcast it on YouTube now. The world sees us – who knows who? Our privacy is shattered! So wrong!".

Now they are really upset and get very quiet.

Steve closes the computer. They walk off the stage with puzzled, upset looks on their faces, shaking their heads.

• •

This scene emphasizes two different issues.

The American Mental Health association has added "selfies" as a mental health addiction. If the selfie activity is done daily and regularly, and a person has their everyday activities interrupted because of the activity, it is considered an addiction.

For example, a 19-year-old teen, Danny in England, was addicted to taking selfies when he was 15. He was known to have taken at least 200 selfies per day. He was considered obsessive compulsive and kept taking the selfies to create a 'perfect' selfie. He became so obsessed with taking them, he attempted to commit suicide when he just could not create the 'perfect' selfie. He dropped out of school and spent nearly ten hours per day taking selfies in an attempt to create a 'perfect' one.

Danny's case has been described as being extreme. To paraphrase a Psychiatrist, Dr. David Veale, who has explained it is not a vanity issue but a mental health issue. Suicide is a threat in this type of addiction. (Addiction.com).

As part of Digital Supervision, parents need to be alert to the uses of the camera selfie option on any digital device, such as cellphone, iPad, camera, video camera – all digital devices and any excessive use of the feature. Prolonged times in private and selfie use, should be avoided. If parents are aware, they need to keep the communication with their children open and inspect the cellphone or other devices on a regular basis to see what pictures might be recorded on it.

This scene gives two different types of scenarios. The second scenario is explained below, and is an example of how a predator can take over a webcam on a digital device. This can be unnerving, as the characters in the play have experienced.

Device users can have a type of malware installed in their machines, without the user having knowledge of it happening. The type of malware being used on the laptop in this case, is a R.A.T, (random or remote access Trojan). The person who installs it, (sometimes called a "ratter") can take over the webcam and actually record what is taking place, if the webcam is not covered.

A couple in Toronto Canada was watching a movie one night in their bedroom. They were streaming a movie using their laptop, located in the bedroom. Eventually, they became intimate and later went to sleep. They woke up in the morning with their intimate exchange being played on You Tube. This was a disturbing experience.

Based on this scene in the play, and the experience of many, it is important to have all digital devices in more public areas of the home, never in the bedroom, and have the webcam covered unless in use. Always cover the webcam when not in use. This is another aspect of Digital Supervision.

SCENE THREE - FACEBOOK (SOCIAL MEDIA) – CLONING, FRIENDS, CRIMINAL INVOLVEMENT

Setting: Two boys, Jake and Steve are on the right side of the stage playing Minecraft in Jake's house. On the other side of the stage are Rhonda and Nancy, at Rhonda's house.

Narrator: Jake and Steve, are gaming, playing Minecraft. They are enjoying the construction they have developed with a highway, 25-story hotel, fencing and other fancy types of landscape.

All of a sudden, message comes through Facebook (social media) to Jake from Claire. Jake is excited because he has tried to date Claire she didn't want to go out with him.

Jake looks at Steve, and says "Claire – wow a message from Claire!! She is awesome. I have wanted to take her out. I am going to accept her friend request." smiles and gives a thumbs up.

Steve rolls his eyes and says "I know what Claire is all about." and gives a thumbs down.

Steve says "I thought you were already a friend of hers."

Jake "Must not be - I don't think so. I will accept the request. It is a first step to going out with her."

Other side of the stage –

Rhonda: "Hey, he accepted the request from Claire! Good. Let's meet him tonight and we can "chat" with him. He won't know the difference. He deserves what he gets."

Nancy: "Perfect. Put in the message that Claire wants to have a coffee at Coffee Culture near his house in Woodstock."

Rhonda: "For sure. Let's see the response."

Jake: "Hey, she wants to go for a coffee with me! I can't believe it. This is a really good chance for me. I am going!. It's right near my house!!!"

Steve: "Wow, I'd be careful if I were you. I am going to go with you to make sure everything is okay. This just doesn't seem right to me."

Jeremy: "Oh, you're just jealous! You don't need to babysit me. She won't think I am much of a man. She wants to meet at 4:00. That's two hours from now."

Steve: "Ok, but let me go with you and I will just stay in the background. At least do that."

Jeremy: "No problem. Just be in the shadows. Be there before I get there."

Steve: "OK. It may be her picture on the Facebook (social media) ID but I am not so sure about this. She really did not want to go out with you before. Why now?"

Rhonda: "Well, he is going to meet us. Then we can let him know about everything and settle the score."

Nancy: "Good. Glad you thought of this."

Jake gets excited and says he would love to get together and wondered where. Claire suggests Williams on Wonderland South. Jake agrees and says he is pleased to see her and get to know her better.

Steve looks at Jeremy and shakes his head. He says "it might not be such a good idea. I know Claire is not interested in you Jake."

All of a sudden, a Facebook friend request comes in on messenger from Claire.

Jake "Hey she just sent me another text and says she is excited to see me. Man, I can't believe it – finally!!"

Steve shrugs his shoulders, looks at Jake, "It should be okay. But,, I will go along and make sure everything is okay"

Jake "Ok. But stay in the background. Don't want her to even know you are there."

· ·

Facebook Cloning is becoming more common. In this scenario, the girls are working on gaining the trust of "Jake". They are doing everything they can to get him to a place where they can exercise the revenge they feel toward him. Jake is unsuspecting of a possible cloning situation.

This has happened and can result in devastating consequences. This is not "hacking". It is a real issue, and is becoming even more of an issue. How is it done? The cloner will access public information from a Facebook account and then proceed to clone the information. Facebook users need to be aware of their security settings and set them so that people cannot access the data unless they are a friend. However, some friends can end up not being "friends".

When the cloned "fake profile" account has been set up (using the actual picture of the person who owns the authentic account), the cloner will then proceed to send friend requests to the original ID friend list. Many people accept a friend request without scrutinizing the request. If users believe they are already a friend of the requesting account, it should be investigated. They may think they were a friend but unfriended them in error; or, they may not remember they were on their friend list.

Once a fake profile clone account is on a Facebook ID, they can then begin accessing friends on ID's for which they have been accepted. Then, the scamming begins.

They will start sending messages to the acquired friends using the cloned ID. Friends will then believe it is legitimate. One scam, is to send a message that they are lost in a foreign country and require funds to get home. Or, the cloned account has won some money and ask the friends if they would like to become a part of the winnings. They are then asked to send money in order to receive the funds.

It is important to keep all Facebook accounts within tight security choices. Hide friend lists. Keep everything for friends only. Instead of having your actual picture on the ID, try using a family pet or other picture so that cloning can be more difficult.

Do a security check often. Who can see your friends list, pictures, and other items on your account. These are details that should be explained to children and teens as part of Digital Supervision.

Crimes that have been attributed to Facebook:

Scams:

There are many scams conducted using Facebook. Example: You may receive notice that you have won a gift card with a link to a popular product. You click the link and proceed to use the gift card to purchase the product but need to use your credit card for a portion of the cost or for shipping. A scammer then has your credit card number and has no doubt recorded your password. If it seems too good to be true, it probably is......

Identity Theft: Too often, people take pictures of the front of their home with the street number on the front. They give the "true" information about their address, birth date, education, number of children and their names, etc. Keep all information private. Facebook profiles should be brief, and in fact, inaccurate. If you live in Toronto or Washington, give a fake city. Be mindful of your information being accessed for the wrong reasons, always.

Defamation, stalking, and harassment:

These are all possibilities through Facebook. The security items are available in Facebook, and other social media, and are important to apply.

It is important that adults use Digital Supervision to communicate to their children that the accounts of their children lack any personal information that could be used against them, and to educate their children about the realities of the environment. Facebook (all social media) is an excellent source of communication between friends and families but also for the dark side and criminals. Learn more about the safety issues to be used throughout this book.

SCENE 4 – SNAPCHAT – 24 HOUR DISAPPEARING CHAT

Setting: Friends, Rhonda and Nancy on the right side of the stage chatting and using Snap Chat with cell phones. On the left side of the stage, friends Steve and Jennifer are doing the same thing. They are chatting, laughing, and having a good time.

Rhonda looks at Nancy and says "I'm taking a weird selfie." She is laughing, screws up her face, and takes the picture.

Nancy takes a look and laughs "Sheesh, you look pretty sick!! Who do you think we should send this one to?."

Rhonda "Hey, I haven't seen Steve in a long time. Let's send it to him!"

Nancy "Absolutely!! Do you have his number?"

Rhonda "Let's see – YES!! Here it is. Sent! Let's see if he says anything!"

Other side of the stage.......

Steve is sitting at the table and takes out his cell phone. Looks at the picture and laughs. "Yes, I'm taking one and sending it back to Rhonda." He makes a weird face laughing and sends it to her.

Jennifer "Lol!! Go for it – what a picture!!"

Rhonda and Nancy start laughing. Nancy "Holy cow what a face lol!! Ask him where he is right now."

Rhonda "Perfect. Texting 'Where are you right now?'" The girls start giggling and waiting for his response.

Nancy looks at the picture "Can't tell where he is. Looks like it's near a body of water."

Steve laughs and texts aloud "As if you want to know! I'm going to take another selfie and let you guess!!"

Jennifer "They'll never guess I bet! Don't know if they have ever been here."

Rhonda and Nancy get the new picture. They look at each other and shrug their shoulders.

Rhonda then says "Hey, I am pretty sure he has the geofilter on his Snapchat. We can figure out where he is by that – he will be shocked."

The girls look on the cell at his location.

Rhonda shouts "he's in Port Dover!!! I can tell by the fries truck in the background!

Nancy "For sure – I was just there two weeks ago. Way ta go Rhonda!!

Rhonda "I am going to text him He'll be so shocked. LOL. This is a riot!"

Steve receives the text, and replies out loud while texting "Hey, you got me!! I am sitting on the beach in Port Dover having their fries and pop! Why don't you come over? The fries are great and the weather super! How did you figure it out? Jennifer is here too!!"

He takes a pic of himself and Jennifer smiling.

Jennifer "Good. Maybe they will come now!"

• •

This scene illustrates the SnapMaps feature in SnapChat, which is managed by the user and has to be turned off and on for it to work. A number of parents have raised concern that their children can be located by anyone on SnapMaps. It is managed by the user. A child should have the feature (geo locator) turned off if their location is an issue to parents.

Predators can be an issue with this feature. If they have befriended a child digitally, they then have a connection with the child. It is also important to note that SnapChat is popular with the younger children, a known invitation for predators.

If they are trying to locate the child without their knowing, they can then use SnapMaps to find out their location at any given time, provided the SnapMaps is active. As a part of Digital Supervision, parents need to be aware of this feature and provide rules for children regarding its use. A general rule should be to have the app inactive unless it is required.

Another feature about SnapChat with predator involvement – when the predator becomes a friend, they can lure a child into sending pictures (nudes) or incriminating information to them. The pictures, etc. can then be used for sextortion. Child pornography predators like the environment because of the erasing feature – texts and pictures will be erased automatically after a time. However, prior to the pictures disappearing, they can do a screen capture so that the picture will be their's forever.

SnapChat has an alarming number of predators involved so the predators can exchange child pornography. As stated earlier, younger children tend to migrate toward SnapChat. Once a predator has 'groomed' a child, the child will send pictures to them because they trust them. It is difficult for law enforcement to investigate incidents because SnapChat deletes pictures and information after a time.

Using Digital Supervision, parents need to be alert to what their children are using and educate them on the dangers of Snapchat. At a young age, this is concerning because the child does not have the maturity level to determine what is safe and who might be at the other end. Young children have either a trust of adults or feel intimidated by adults. In either case, it is problematic without an adult practicing Digital Supervision to guide the child.

SCENE 5 - CHATTING, PASSWORDS, ONLINE PROFILES, AND HOLIDAYS

Setting: Two friends, Rhonda and Nancy on the right side of the stage on a laptop using Facebook and Twitter. Two brothers, Shane and Jason, are on the left side of the stage on a laptop using Facebook. Rhonda is on her Facebook site. She is quite excited because her family is going to Disneyworld in Florida tomorrow for two weeks.

Rhonda is with Nancy and says she is posting on Facebook "Hey everybody. I am super excited. I am going to Las Vegas tomorrow with my family. We will be there for two weeks. Eat your hearts out!!!"

Nancy "Where are you staying? I have heard Prince Harry went to Las Vegas!"

Rhonda "don't know! Just going with my parents and brother. The whole family is going."

Nancy "What are you doing with your dog? A Doberman must be hard to place."

Rhonda "At my grandmothers. She loves the dog. I am so excited."

Nancy "Wish I could go too. It is supposed to be a great place to go. Are you sure you should be telling everyone?"

Rhonda "Of course. We can see just how jealous everyone is. If they don't say like or something, we will know lol!"

Other side of the stage, two brothers, Shane and Jason, are reading the posts. They give each other the thumbs up and nod. One of the boys is an unknown friend. He read the post on Rhonda's Facebook. He smiles. He now knows her house will be empty for two weeks and he will be able to go in and take things.

Shane "Hey man – they're going to be away. I know we can get into their place."

Jason "You sure you know all that? I don't want to get caught."

Shane "Yeh – look on their picture gallery. They have a picture of the front of the house. Their house sign has the number and street. Piece of cake man!"

Jason "Right – they are in Tillsonburg. Wow – sitting ducks!"

Shane "I know! People don't get how easy it is to find stuff out about them on Facebook and social media. I want that stereo and TV in that picture."

Jason "Perfect – how about in two nights after they leave? The neighbours forget they are gone and we can go in without a problem. Bet they have a night light on too lol!"

Shane "Definitely – we will go at about 2 a.m. and be really quiet. Wednesday, everyone goes to work the next morning and will be asleep."

Jason "Cool. Glad you got your own car."

The family is on their holiday for two weeks. The laptop is gone from the other side of the stage. When they arrive.....

Rhonda "Oh no!!!!! Our house has been robbed! I hope my laptop is still here. The laptop!! I can't believe our house was robbed! Awful!! Who would have done this?"

Nancy "I kind of think it might have been your post on Facebook before you left. I would have posted after I got back. What do you think?"

Rhonda "I don't know but don't mention it to my parents. They would be so angry. We have lost everything."

Nancy "You have to call the police."

Rhonda "I know all of my Facebook friends. None of them would do such a thing."

Nancy "Don't be so sure Rhonda."

• •

This is another example of how Social Media can be used to commit crime. I have been in contact with several people who have had such an experience.

How many times have you seen pictures of families on a plane on their way to a vacation? It is posted in present, real time, with the time and day broadcast. Do you think everyone will be able to determine that they are away and their house is probably empty? Of course.

In this scene, the boys reviewing the Facebook ID noticed items in the pictures that would be excellent to take. They knew where the family lived because there is a picture of the front of their house with the street number; they also have their town in their

Facebook profile. In addition, they were "known" to the family – a situation that is disturbing because they were "supposed" to be friends.

It is important to share with children that digital "friends" are not always "friends". Or, their connections can be looking for chances to engage in criminal activity. In this case, the known friends ended up to be criminals.

SCENE 6 - CELL PHONES

Setting: Three friends, Rhonda, Nancy and Steve on the right side of the stage sharing pictures and chatting through their cell phones. On the left side of the stage, is the father of Rhonda, Ron.

Rhonda, Nancy and Steve are texting each other and sharing a few jokes through their cell phones. They talk as they text.

Nancy: "Hey get this text!! Steve wants to go to the liquor store and get some stuff!"

Rhonda: "LOLOLOLOL! Ask him how are we going to get it? We are all under age." Nancy texts Steve back. "How are we getting it?"

Steve: "I have ways my friends." He texts another one.

Nancy: "Hey, I am sure your brother wouldn't buy anything for us. He is really careful because of your Dad."

Rhonda: "I know – so am I. I am really careful. I can't text Steve because Dad mirrors my cell phone. It is a real pain."

Nancy: "Really. So, he knows all of your texts?"

Rhonda "Yes. He is so controlling. I will email Steve using the email address my Dad doesn't know about lol! I can get around the mirroring that way – he doesn't get copies of that email. I will just say I am going to study at your house and then go to the dance. It will be a blast! I do it all the time!."

Steve sends another text to Nancy about the dance at the school the next day. They are all in Grade 11.

Rhonda: "Hey Nancy, I am going to the dance for sure. Anyone else going that we know?"

Nancy: "All of our friends. We will have lots of fun!"

Meanwhile, Rhonda's father, Ron, is checking out her cell phone. He has her emails copied to his phone and can check out her activity any time. He also mirrors her cell phone to his.

Rhonda is aware of the cell phone mirroring and that her father receives copies of her emails. He is on a break from work and wants to make sure his daughter is following the rules. He sees the texts and thinks they are harmless.

Ron says to himself: "Gee Rhonda. You're doing alright." He checks out her emails, and sees that she has not sent an email today at all.

Ron talks to himself "Wow, she is going to study tomorrow night. Nancy is such a great kid. Way to go Rhonda."

Steve: "Okay. See you girls tomorrow. I have a friend in Ingersoll and we can get the stuff at the Domino's pizza strip mall. No one will know and I will be back in Woodstock for the dance."

Nancy: "Good. None of us want anyone knowing though so let's just be careful. You sure your father doesn't know about this email account? I will text Steve back and make sure he doesn't text or email you then."

Rhonda: "Absolutely. Tell Steve for sure. The stuff I have sent people Dad would have a fit over if he knew about my other email account lol"

Steve sends another email asking Nancy if they would like to party at Stan's after the dance. Stan's parents are away and they can have a fantastic time.

Nancy: "Yeh!! Count us in! Steve said there is a party at Stan's after the dance. Let's put the word out on FB and all chats. It will be packed!"

Rhonda: "I am just going to tell Dad I am studying at your house for an exam."

All three start laughing and give each other the thumbs up.

Ron, Rhonda's father, checks out her cell phone again.

Thinking out loud - Ron: "I know something is up but I can't figure it out. I know Rhonda too well. Her texts don't indicate too much. I worry about her. I guess I will have to believe she is studying for now."

• •

Parents can mirror a cell phone so that all activity on the phone of their child is recorded to their phone.

To mirror a phone, a parent has to download the app for such a purpose. Parents can also have the child's email copied to them so they can check on the content of their child's email for child protection.

Rhonda has a second cell phone. Her father is unaware of the second phone. She also has a separate Facebook account, using a different Gmail ID. A person can create several email accounts. When I was teaching, students used to laugh about parents thinking their emails were copied to them. They always had a "friend" email account of which their parents were unaware.

Rhonda's second cell phone is referred to as a "burner" phone. Read in later chapters the details of a "burner" phone.

There are other ways of monitoring children, which should be considered by parents, and is in the remainder of this book.

CHAPTER 5

CODE WORDS FOR CHILD SAFETY

Parents have been advised to tell their children a code word or phrase for the child to use to determine if a person who approaches them is a "safe" person. For example, a parent may say the code word is "hockey". If the person picking the child up knows the code word, then the child will go with the adult without further question.

Digital Supervision application:

Do you believe this is the safest way to protect your child?

The code-word system is viewed as a safe method. Initially, this is advisable, and I agree. However, more factors must be considered when implementing child protection. We are in the digital age and child protection must be modernized.

In many cases, children have been taught to feel safe with family members and friends of the family. Unfortunately, in many cases, an abductor or abuser falls within the category of a "known friend". A code word could be ineffective in such cases.

According to data provided by Statistics Canada related to sexual offences committed toward children:

- Approximately nine in ten (88%) were committed by someone known to the victim;
- the rest (12%) were committed by a stranger to the child.
- Of the "known" acquaintances, 44% was an acquaintance of the family/victim; 38% was a family member; and 6% were by an intimate partner of a parent.
- Children of a younger age were mainly victimized by a family member.
- For ages 0 to 3, a family member was charged 66% of the time (two thirds).
- In fact, most sexual abuse of children occurs in private residences.
- Most sexual offenders are male, although females do offend. [6]

These are the KNOWN cases. Unfortunately, too often, cases are unknown, either because of the age of the victim or the fear instilled in the victim by the predator. Children rarely talk about the trauma because of the effectiveness of the grooming of the predator. Fear takes over.

Based on data, parents, guardians, and professional allies, need to consider safety from all perspectives. The code word should be applied with family members as well; in other words, when picking up a child, a code word should be used regardless of relationship.

Another example, parents often post pictures of their children online through Facebook and other social media. They give countless details of their children. There is often a picture of the child in front of the family dwelling for the first day of school. Sound familiar? All of us have witnessed this type of post. The second picture will be of the child either walking to school or in front of the school. The parent will post a detailed paragraph about the child and how nervous or excited they were to go to school. Also, that they like the teacher and name the teacher.

What parents may not realize, is that there is an unknown on their media friends list or they have made all posts public. Even worse, a known friend could be a predator lurking within their friend circle under the façade of a "good" person.

The person witnessing the post then has the picture of the child, picture of the family dwelling, picture of the school, and details about the personality of the child. What is to keep this person from going to the school to pick up the child from the playground? As a former teacher, I know there are spaces on playgrounds at recess and lunch hour that will be more open while the children are at play. It may not be difficult for someone to approach a child within that environment.

A predator then goes to your child and says "Your Mom told me you were excited to go to school and couldn't sleep last night. She asked me to come and get you so that I could help you with your dreams. I guess your Dad, "Bill", is worried about you too."

Do you think your child would then go with the predator? At this point, a child could trust them because the person knows so much about them.

This predator could be a known, an unknown, or a family member. What do you do?

It is important, as part of Digital Supervision, that parents exercise caution at all times regarding data shared about their children and family. There is an inherent urge for parents to post many pictures of their children on social media. It seems to be highly competitive for parents to do so. Avoid this urge. The safety of your children depends on it.

I have spoken to many parents who have believed they are not "good" parents because they do not have pictures of their children for the social media "brag". Please be advised, that NOT posting pictures should never be seen as a negative choice.

CHAPTER 6

CHILD ON CHILD SEXUAL ASSAULT

The Internet has too much information that is readily available. Earlier, I cited statistics related to pornography and that over 80% of children are exposed to unsolicited pornography.

There are children experimenting sexually because of what they have viewed. I have had parents asking me if I believe their children are experimenting sexually at the age of six because of the Internet. It is NOT normal for children to experiment at young ages with sexual knowledge that is beyond their years. Often, children experiment with viewing themselves nude but it is not common that children will practice with penetration, using objects and other modes of physical contact.

One parent called and told me her son and daughter were at their grandparent's house. When they were hiding behind the couch, and the grandparents were tending to the farm, the son asked the daughter to get naked and kiss his penis. The daughter was five and the son seven. Again, this is NOT normal behaviour.

According to Heidi Olson, sexual assault nurse examiner (SANE), Kansas City, USA, the accessibility of pornography on the Internet may be causing the majority of child-on-child sexual assault. Children are seeing pornography and re-enacting what they see on the screen. She reported that some parents have returned home and found siblings in sexual positions hoping to be like the adults in the movies. The SANE data describe children as being exposed to porn at very early ages (four and five).

Further, the SANE team determined that perpetrators of child-on-child assaults are commonly between the ages of eleven and fifteen, and that just about half of the perpetrators are minors.[7]

In The Guardian, UK, it was recorded from police reports that over 30,000 cases of child-on-child sexual assaults were reported in 2019, and that child-on-child sexual assaults have soared. [8]

This opens a new type of challenge for parents. How are they going to cope with this type of behaviour? The greatest asset for parents is to practice Digital Supervision. They need open communication with their children, particularly when it comes to the accidental discovery of pornography.

Olson states that children should not be villainized for being on porn. It is not their fault. We need to discuss the problem and be open with our children. To take away a computer and privileges because of it, is villainizing our children, which is unfortunate. There should be more controls of information. Some have gone so far as to state there should be no pornography accessible over the Internet, and I agree. At least, have no "free" pornography online. Because so much of it is free, children are able to access it any time.

Humanity supervising humanity must be practiced. Prior to the digital age, it was the practice. Online child protection requires parents and supervising adults to take charge of the Internet in their homes and digital devices. We cannot depend on computers, computer filters, and digital devices to do our digital parenting and supervision for us. Unfortunately, the majority of parents avoid using filters or supervision of any kind.

Filters are advisable, particularly in the younger ages. However, as children mature, they are able to bypass some filters and parents need to be alert to this reality. There is a new filter using Artificial Intelligence which sections the Internet into a "Bright Web" that is advisable for purchase. When the child is in the Bright Web, they will not have access to questionable material. Digital Supervision is necessary and should be considered as being interdependent with the filter. When children are engaged in gaming, chats, email, Digital Supervision is necessary. The filter can only do so much in blocking content and behaviours. Parents cannot depend on hardware or software for full child protection online, and are cautioned to avoid a false sense of security.

Without the Bright Web filter, younger children may be able to bypass a different type of filter if they are advised by older siblings. Face it, if your four or five-year-old sees porn, their innocence is over. Also realize, you may be unaware because children will not share this type of exposure with a parent. They inherently realize they might be in trouble for seeing it. Again, Olson's suggestion that the child should not be villainized is important guidance for parents to follow.

The flip side of this situation, is that a child may be accessing pornography on their own, based on conversations with other children or predators. This situation requires a whole new type of conversation. Parents need to ask children how they found the pornography, if someone directed them (friend or unknown on the Internet), was it at another home (a friends or adults). The conversation goes to a different level if a predator is suspected. If addiction to pornography has developed, professional therapy would be required in most cases.

True story: I had a parent come to me with a concern about her son's online activities. When she investigated the browser history, she discovered he had been on several xxx porn sites. It caused her great anxiety.

She removed the digital device from her son and told him to never go there again. It is important to keep communications open with children.

The parent discussed the situation with the child and asked him where he got the idea to look at XXX sites. The child responded by saying "friends told me to go there to view 'funny pictures". The parents were distraught about this because they had provided the device. After speaking with the mother, I asked her if she thought the idea came from children at school or perhaps some other source. She didn't know what to believe.

Through my own experience as a survivor of child sexual abuse (teacher when I was at the age of 15), I explained to the mother that the chances were that a child did not offer the idea to her son. Children would more than likely suggest her son view naked pictures of adults, etc. A 'predator' would ask if a child wanted to see some 'funny' pictures. The predator would more than likely not use the word 'naked' because it could alert a child they may be doing something wrong and that a parent would not be pleased. Children are usually told not to walk around naked.

At the ages of 15 (high school) and 21 (university), I was sexually assaulted by a teacher and then a professor. The details are in a later chapter. At no time, did either man ask to have sex, ask to have permission to touch my body, nor anything else. One asked to be silly; the other just began his assault. Both predators were in a position of authority, a dominant figure.

With these two unfortunate experiences, I can safely say predators are RARELY open with their intentions with a victim.

With the child previously mentioned, 'funny' pictures point to a predator grooming a child, not a friend telling him to go to certain websites. As explained earlier, predators often introduce pornography in their quest to gain the trust of a victim.

It is important, as part of Digital Supervision, that parents know and understand the grooming process and try to discern if a child is a victim of grooming. Open lines of communications must be clear with children. If you explain the difference between appropriate pictures and inappropriate pictures, (good pictures, bad pictures) children will then feel it is 'okay' to discuss online experiences, such as these, openly with parents. If not, a child can feel traumatized, and alienated from their parents because of their secret. Some children have lost sleep and change behaviours because of viewing pornography.

Predators groom and emphasize "secrets". With Digital Supervision, this knowledge for an adult must be learned and realized, for the sake of child protection. In these cases, knowledge is definitely power. Without open communication, negative behaviours can develop, such as child on child sexual assault.

Heidi Olson, believes child on child sexual assault is in epidemic proportions, and becoming a public health crisis. This type of trauma can have life-long results. Both parents and children are traumatized. Again, Olson believes the main source of this sexual behaviour is exposure via screens.

Open discussion with children about possible content on the Internet as well as open discussion if children view pornographic content should be practiced. Without the open discussion, the dialogue will not take place and children will be left to their own means with possible child on-child sexual assault, or, in the case of violence in pornography, child-on-child violent sexual assault. It is important parents and other adults realize that discussion be "cautious" and to avoid prompting any curiosity related to a child seeking inappropriate sites and pornography. This is a situation unique to families and the types of children involved. Advice is being given, however, the relationship between parents and children is always unique and needs to be respected when dealing with such "difficult" situations.

CHAPTER 7

THE DARK WEB

There are three levels of the Internet:

The surface level – where most citizens are operating on the Internet. It is a low-maintenance, less secure environment.

The Deep Web – in this section, a secure login is required. For example, government workers, law enforcement, bankers, and others.

The Dark Web – This is a section that provides anonymity for the user. The IP address of the machine is not identifiable which provides the anonymity in browsing. Police use the IP address for tracing a machine where illegal activity has been detected. It is difficult to trace activity in the Dark Web, even for law enforcement.

Some cases:

Some spouses have found child pornography on the home computer or cell phone of their spouse. They realize the pictures or videos had to have been put on the device by their spouse. They worry that their children might see the pictures or videos.

This is a difficult situation for a spouse. Often, the spouse decides they really do not know their spouse at all. It becomes stressful. They do not want to contact the authorities because of what it could do to their family.

Some wives have contacted me to talk about their home situation and to obtain advice. It has been difficult for the wives to share their personal stories. They were frightened they could be charged for possession of child pornography themselves. They become outraged when they think their children might have seen the pictures or videos, if the device has been shared throughout the family. Regardless, the police should be notified. Children would have been assaulted and harmed in the pictures. If you knowingly are in possession of child pornography, that becomes a whole different conversation.

It is important to note the date and time the pictures were saved to the device. It will determine who, in a household, might be responsible for the download of material. It will also determine if a person in the household has actually produced the pictures or videos, which is a more problematic situation. If you have investigated and found the victim is a child in your home, therapy and counselling should be sought for the child, and the police notified immediately.

To go further, parents, caregivers, and professionals need to be aware of the details of the "Dark" web in order to fully realize the need for Digital Supervision in cases where there is suspicious activity.

When on a search engine while using a Dark Web Browser (Tor, Subgraph OS, Waterfox, Tails, Opera, Whonix, Invisible Internet Project {a 12P browser}), the tracks of the browsing activity will be anonymous. What does this mean? The person who has installed the browser to engage in surfing the Dark Web knows exactly what they are doing. They want anonymity with their Internet activities. The IP address is anonymous. Tracing the offending computer and IP address is difficult.

Never hesitate to contact the police regarding this type of activity if criminal behaviour is detected on a Dark Web browser. There could be a child somewhere that is suffering, or your child involved with the Dark Web could be putting themselves in danger.

Anyone in this section of the Internet is usually not there for a positive purpose, although journalists use it for anonymity in reporting. The type of crimes being committed in the Dark Web can range from child pornography, to arms sales, drug deals, terrorism, and many other crimes. A number of predators use the Dark Web to protect their criminal activity.

As part of Digital Supervision, awareness of the different browsers on our devices is necessary. Their presence can indicate a far sinister issue than just going on the Internet and enjoying the many "good" things it has to offer.

In some cases, people can use a VPN, Virtual Private Network, to browse. This is not a Dark Web browser situation. Often, people who travel use VPN's in order to avoid any type of infiltration of their data while on the road. VPN's do not provide anonymity but they do provide a more secure channel to access the Internet. If there is a VPN on your device, your

IP (Internet Protocol) address for your device will be changed as you access the Internet. VPN's are often used for corporate computers if employees are on the road and they require better security.

I have had parents tell me their children (under 18 or adults) are using the Dark Web "just to see what it is all about". This is a dangerous activity. We need to realize whenever there is a connection out of our computer, there can be a connection coming back in for which we are unaware. If you are a parent (or homeowner), and you realize someone within your home is engaged with the Dark Web, you should become suspicious of their activities. If you pay for the Internet, the gateway to the Dark Web that is being accessed, becomes a greater issue.

CHAPTER 8

DEVICE MONITORING

The greatest advice given to parents has been to have a computer in the open area of the home. Parents have dutifully moved their computer to a living room, family room, kitchen or other area of the home. This will work if parents have a certain amount of computer literacy, and, if they actually look at the computer screen while the child is engaged in activity. Too often, parents put the device in the common area and rarely watch what a child is doing. The child knows when the parent is entering the room; or, the ability or lack of ability of the parent on a digital device.

Unfortunately, too many parents have little knowledge of what their child might be doing and even how to investigate the activity of the child on a device. In this case, knowledge is definitely power.

Would you give your child a car to drive without a license? Would you want your child driving around your city without you in the car? Would your insurance company want this situation? Of course not!

We have to realize that the Internet enables your child to drive around the world without you at their side. Digital Supervision is designed to help you supervise your child in order to protect them.

As soon as parents provide a gateway to the Internet from their home, they have increased their responsibilities as a parent, exponentially. I stress to all audiences – just because there is a digital screen, and you think your children know more than you do, does not relieve you of parental responsibilities for a minor.

When a router is installed in a home, a computer filter needs to be added to the equipment. The filter will help filter content coming into the home, which is necessary. The negative side of using a filter? Parents become dependent and believe the technology is doing the whole job.

The filter is a piece of hardware that is installed between the router (device that supplies the gateway to the Internet) and the computer. The filter helps to separate desirable websites and information, from the less desirable. This can be described in comparison to email. All email services provide a filter. If you have had to refer to a spam file folder, the email service has "filtered" the information you have received to eliminate unwanted email. A hardware filter does the same, but filters out unwanted websites and information.

There are mobile device filters available that have minimal effectiveness because children learn how to work around the filter. There are also mobile device carriers that offer blocking for an extra fee.

Some filters will give a report to parents as to the surfing being done on the Internet. Filters can only do some of the job. Parents must engage in Digital Supervision in order to keep children protected.

However, Digital Supervision is required because filters will not give a report on chats, possible accidental discovery of pornography on a seemingly "benign" website, exposure to cyberbullying, exposure to hate, predator involvement, and more.

Gaming systems are not covered through a filter. When gaming, the communication is done through the server of the game. If a child is on an X-Box gaming system, they will be playing online with "anyone". This is a safe haven for predation. Predators have asked children to purchase headphones so they can chat with them without anyone in the household having knowledge.

Most gaming systems have a geographic locator on the system, facilitating augmented reality (the technology that supports the Pokemon Go game and other games).

Many parents wonder what a "geolocator" is and the implications. With the use of geolocator, a person's location might be seen across social media. Cell phones are particularly sensitive to this feature. If the geolocator is turned off, a person could move about without location being known. However, if parents are familiar with geolocator, they may want the feature on (particularly on a cell phone) so they might be able to locate their child if they are late coming home, or if they might be missing.

The safety of a child depends on who is on their friend list. There is a competition among many children (adults included) to have multiple friends on their list. With this type of competition comes the risk of having people who are not true "friends".

As part of Digital Supervision, parents must have open communication with their children and guide them as to safe choices on lists of friends and sharing of information. In the scenes from the play in earlier chapters, the ease with which children innocently share information was illustrated.

Live streaming is possible. Predators love this because they can see the child they are communicating with and avoid police intervention. Often, they will turn off their own video and only see the child. They will be viewed by the child through a taped video. This type of communication can be dangerous because the child can be groomed, with the predator viewing reactions and facial expressions. They can then begin asking the child to send pictures or to undress for them, after the grooming process is at an advanced stage.

Digital Supervision is necessary to discuss with the child who is gaming with them, what to do and not to do under different circumstances. It is also advisable to game with your child, ask them questions about their game, how to play it, goals within the game, parts of the gaming system, and other details. It is difficult to supervise if you are unaware of the game and system. Learn the system details before giving it to you child to operate.

Type of online games:

Web games and apps – These games can be played through specific websites or an application that is downloaded onto a mobile phone. A number of these games can be played through social media.

Console games – These are played through gaming systems such as Xbox, PlayStation or Nintendo systems. They are connected to TVs with games being purchased at stores.

Mobile games – games played using a mobile phone, after being downloaded to a cell phone.

Handheld games – iPad, specific gaming device. These systems can host online games.

The issues with online gaming could be inappropriate content, predator gamers, bullying by gamers, grooming for nude pictures, grooming for meetups, violent gamers, vindictive gamers, and more. There are games and systems that can be played offline on a computer or other devices, a safer situation, and one which would be benign to predation and other negative behaviours.

With online gaming, parental controls are available on gaming systems and it is important to study them and put blocks on the system. Age ratings for games a child is playing should be noted prior to children engaging in playing the game. However, keep in mind, predators will go to games where the child is the most naïve and innocent. Most games require age 13 or older but younger children may be on games for their own age group and older. If under the age of 13, online gaming should be avoided.

Children should be advised to not share personal information or pictures while gaming. Define personal information – age, location, address, where parents work, full name, school, vacations, colour of hair, height, weight, colour of eyes – anything that could define who and where a child is located.

Dr. R. Dyson, Ed.D., has studied gaming in detail. Her research has included the effects of violence in gaming on gamers. She emphasizes the gaming culture tends to be a threat to global stability.

She quotes different game examples in her writings. Lte. Col. Dave Grossman has researched that specific games can be blamed for the rise in mass homicides globally.

Unfortunately, millions of children are being trained at an early age that "killing" is fun, and just a game. They even emphasize the type of shooting to use. As Dyson points out, "only a very small fraction of murderers shoot victims in the head or face. It is also rare amongst soldiers in battle." [9] And, our children are playing these games, shooting people in the face and other body parts, over and over again.

On top of predation in the gaming environments, parents need to consider the types of activities their children are involved with on a daily basis using gaming devices.

Related to predators and "grooming", there is additional information in the next chapter. Parents and adult allies need to be alert to the types of behaviours associated with gaming and addictions to them.

CHAPTER 9

DETAILS ABOUT GROOMING

There is a process used by predators referred to as "grooming", which has been done traditionally in person (and still is), but more often now, done online. This is trying to gain the trust of their intended victim, as well as the family and friends of the victim. In my family, a member was being groomed at the age of four. We have always wondered how this could happen. I advise everyone, grooming includes everyone, especially the parents and siblings. The predator does everything in their power to have all parties involved "trust" them.

There are different stages of grooming, usually in this order, but not necessarily:

<u>Friendship forming stage</u> – gaining trust.

Predators are good at what they do, which is why Digital Supervision must include discussion with children about online and offline friends. Online communications are particularly important because we rarely "see" the exchanges taking place.

A predator will begin communicating with the intended victim. They will ask the child questions about their family, where they live, are they happy with their parents and siblings – anything they can use to gain trust and provide communication with the child that will help them identify with the child.

I asked a ten-year-old child once if they gamed online. The response was "yes". I then asked them who gamed with them. The child mentioned two friends' names. I asked if any grownups gamed with them. The child seemed surprised and said "yeh, this older guy. Really nice guy." I remained calm and stated that it is unusual for an older person to play with a ten-year-old. I asked the child if the older person had a ten-year-old son. The child was shocked and said "yeh, how did you know?". Of course the predator had a ten-year-old son – finding something in common with the intended victim.

I share this story with children when speaking in schools. They are always shocked and begin to realize the reality of who might be at the other end of a gaming environment.

This previous situation is a true story, and a good example of how predators try to gain trust. They find things in common with a child to get that trust. A trusting child would know no different. Unfortunately, most parents would see this as a benign situation as well. A ten-year-old son too? Common response.

The second stage is development of a relationship. The above example is one way – finding things in common. They will then ask if the child is having difficulty at home with parents or siblings. Do they have friends. Then they will start forming an alliance with the child as their new, trusted friend.

They may also befriend the parents and say they will help them out of financial hardship, do things to solve other issues, babysit, and the like. The parents then trust the person because they have needs fulfilled and think the person is great because of it. Online, this could be giving money to the parent, looking after children (babysitting, taking them to shows), just chatting with a parent who might be in a bad relationship, marriage, work, and other examples.

The next stage would be a risk assessment. How are they going to be able to communicate with the child and have them keep the "secrets"? They will ask the child if their parents are around all of the time while they game. Do they have rules about chatting on line? Do they get angry if they are on the computer for too long? They will ask who else uses the computer or the system on which they are chatting (gaming, iPad, etc.). They will also wonder how much parents monitor what is going on with the online activity of the child. The answers to these questions will gauge whether the predator will proceed with further grooming and communication with the child.

Isolating the child from others – the predator knows their secret will not last long if the child isn't trained to only communicate with them and trust only them. At this point, the child is confused but open to conversation with the predator that would be against the rest of their family and friends. The predator is doing what they can to ensure that only *they* should be trusted and only *they* are the best friend a child can have. On line, they could begin asking the child to send pictures in various stages of undress. They may ask the child to open the webcam so that they can see them but the predator may explain their webcam is having a problem so that the predator cannot be seen.

The predator will begin desensitizing the child sexually. They may send pornography and tell them it is normal and to enjoy it. Then, sexuality becomes the main focus and further requests will be made.

The final stage is full control. The predator wants to maintain the relationship with the child and begins asking if the child is able to meet, are the parents aware of anything, have parents been asking questions, is the secret still safe, can you send them some nudes.

Through communications with a child, Digital Supervision should be used. Warning signs a child may be in a negative situation could be:

- Excessive time on the Internet and insisting they be given the time and freedom. When refusal is given by parents, they can erupt into great anger;

- Keeping everything to themselves regarding their online activities and information about their communications with friends;
- Turning the screen off as soon as an adult enters the room (if this happens, the adult should go to the screen and turn it on immediately to see what is going on);
- Using language of a sexual nature that is beyond their age level. Keep in mind this type of language can be learned on a playground too – parents know their children and when this type of verbiage or behaviour is abnormal based on their daily communications;
- Possible isolation from the family for no good reason.

These types of situations can be difficult to determine. However, Digital Supervision must be evident in the home with open communications with children about online activities, rules regarding time online, and parental guidance.

CHAPTER 10

"CYBERBULLICIDE" AND NUDES

Cyberbullicide (Cyberbulling):

Cyberbullicide is more common among youth, but is also used by adults. Bullying has been in existence for centuries. However, now bullying is done using technology, and can be difficult to detect if parents are not practicing Digital Supervision.

There are so many vehicles online that can be used for this purpose - through voice or texting chats on social media, gaming chats, YouTube, augmented reality (AR), virtual reality (VR) and more. Through research and studies, estimates of the number of students who have experienced cyberbullying vary, but it is safe to say, up to 37% between the ages of 12 and 17 have experienced the victimization, with 30% having it happen more than once. Girls are more commonly victims, and involved as "cyberbully perpetrators", than boys.[10]

Unfortunately, most of it is done anonymously through fake emails, and, many people online - once they see the cyberbullying, get involved because they see it as 'fun'. The latter group are particularly dangerous because the victim can be unknown to them.

The victim wonders who is doing the bullying and becomes even more distraught when they cannot even identify the origin of the data being distributed. In that the majority of all teens are online, usually unsupervised, this is a disturbing trend. Too often, it is easy to hide behind a screen and send texts that are cruel and damaging. And, as said earlier, the texts may be sent to a complete unknown from the sender, which becomes even more disturbing.

A part of cyberbullicide includes youth taking pictures of peers that cause severe distress to the target(s) (nudes or sexual encounters). Some teens take pictures of their friends having sex at a party and distribute the pictures online. These types of pictures can result in charges being laid. This is referred to as "sexting", however, sexting can, and is used, to bully others.

Through an oral interview with a parent of a 17-year old youth in Ontario, Canada, their child was found guilty of producing and distributing child pornography because she took pictures of her friends having sex at a party and posted them on Facebook. Her friends were under the age of 18. One parent thought it was just a joke; the other did not. The Criminal Code in most countries outline the activity as a crime and not a joke. In fact, in Canada, it is illegal to share an intimate picture of an adult without their consent, which applies to children as well.

It is unfortunate the 17-year-old now has a criminal record for something that should have been covered in parental Digital Supervision, *proactively.* In some countries, these types of offences will cause a person to be placed on the sex offender registry for life, a minor or not.

In some cases, revenge porn is a part of this type of cyberbullying. Several youths have been charged with this type of offence. Unfortunately, such behaviour has caused numerous suicides. Digital Supervision would help to keep this type of situation supervised and under control by parents. Remember – youth and children have not developed emotionally enough to understand the extreme situations that can occur because of cyberbullying.

Child pornography is neither an accident nor a game. It is a crime. The Criminal Code of most countries is clear: anyone under the age of 18 is considered a child. Therefore, any pictures of nude children, and or of a sexually exploitive nature, may be interpreted as child pornography by law enforcement.

There are thousands of "nudes" in circulation on cell phones and on other devices. These are referred to as "self-exploitive" pictures. Through oral interviews, school Superintendents, Directors, Principals and teachers, the situation has been described as being of epidemic proportions. Because of today's mobile technology and the Internet, the self-exploitive activity has a proliferation of which they have never seen before in their careers. The police have had to discuss this situation with children as young as eight. Digital Supervision would help to avoid this type of meeting with police.

In some cases, in Canada, the Youth Criminal Justice Act has been applied. In other cases, youths have been tried in adult court. Some of the investigations have taken place in the school system. Youth believe they are untouchable if it happens in a school setting. This attitude is being challenged by law enforcement.

Many students have regrets regarding their self-exploitive conduct (taking nudes of themselves and sharing). They realize, too late, that their pictures will be in cyber space forever. (The picture) is out there forever. Unfortunately, the Internet does not forget.

Relationships for teens and children can change many times before they graduate from high school and after graduation. All children need to be educated regarding relationships, usual lack of longevity, and the vulnerable nature of their relationships. Too often, a partner in a relationship agrees to share a nude or intimate picture with their partner because they believe they are "in love" and it will "last forever". This illusion is often shattered and the picture has been shared by a former partner.

Parents need to educate their children regarding "love" relationships in school. Children and youth need to be careful about sharing their activities, information, or images, both in person and digitally. Digital data will outlast personal relationships.

If a child, youth, parent, caregiver, or adult ally is aware of a location of an embarrassing, humiliating or harassing picture, they are advised to go to the website www.needhelpnow.ca. The website has counselors who can assist a family or youth individually, related to the needed emotional care when this occurs. The personnel on the website can also help to remove the unwanted picture from a specific location online. For example, if the picture is on a specific social media site, they will assist in removal. However, if the picture has been shared with many people and is on the Internet in unknown locations, this becomes an impossible task. The best decision is to never share a self-exploitive picture.

It is important to provide here some statistics about children/youth that should be shared with them to emphasize the degree to which intimate pictures are shared. This is referred to as "sexting". These statistics are based on data related to a school environment:

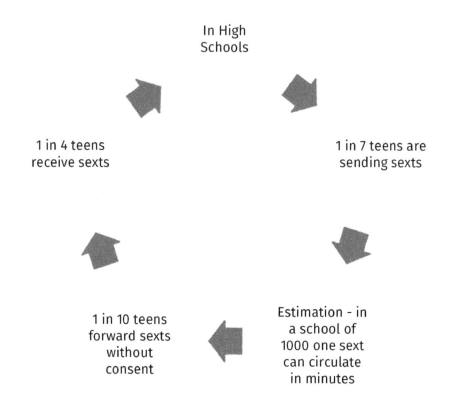

In High Schools

1 in 4 teens receive sexts

1 in 7 teens are sending sexts

1 in 10 teens forward sexts without consent

Estimation - in a school of 1000 one sext can circulate in minutes

In January 2018, police in Châteauguay, near Montreal, Canada, began a campaign and titled it "sexts are porn". The campaign was targeting 12- to 17-year-old children. Police forces around the world are beginning to warn parents that they may be charged if the devices they own and pay for contain nudes of children.

Consensual teen sexting is still considered child pornography under the law of most countries, provided that the country views children under the age of 18 as children. Many people wonder if it is more girls than boys, but statistics have proven that it is more of a balanced issue with girls and boys both participating.

One Detective Superintendent, Susie Harper, Canada has cautioned parents that if a child's mobile phone contract is in the name of the parents, the parent can be liable for the content on the device.

This could cause a search warrant for the parental home to determine if there is illegal content on other digital devices.

When I present, I have had parents tell me they believe that investigating the cell phones and other devices of their children is an "invasion" of the child's privacy. If you are in a position that the police find child pornography on a device registered in your name, you may face a search warrant for your home, which will be an invasion of YOUR privacy. What would be your choice as far as investigating the cellphone of your child under these circumstances?

My question to parents is this – is it _evasion or invasion_? Is it evasion of parental responsibilities or invasion of your child's privacy? Is it rules for the protection of a child? Or is it evasion of parental responsibilities out of fear of reprisal from a child?

Be careful that you practice Digital Supervision and not evasion of parental rights. We have rights as parents – be sure to remember this. Our children have the right to guidance and protection. Invasion of privacy? Evasion vs invasion? No. Protection and instilling good choices with our children should be of paramount importance.

CHAPTER 11

PERSONAL BODY SAFETY

This topic was introduced earlier. It is important to discuss this further in order to give a full understanding of implications.

Parents, caregivers, and professionals might, and should, teach children about personal body safety. This is a multicultural challenge. Different cultures will approach the education of personal body safety in different ways. I am suggesting methods of a global nature. Various cultures will need to adapt to these methods within their own parameters.

One method to begin to describe personal body safety is to explain to children that body parts covered by a bathing suit or clothing are considered "personal" and not to allow others to see them, to touch them, nor take pictures of them without "personal" body parts covered.

Telling children not to allow touching on their personal body parts by another person is important. However, it is equally important to tell children not to touch another person in those body parts either.

In all of the horrendous pictures I have seen of child pornography, no child was being touched with hands. Nor, was the child touching someone with their hands. Other body parts were used. Use your imagination. It becomes problematic when parents say not to allow anyone to touch them. The child assumes that it is with hands. Clarification is necessary. "No touching" should include no touching with hands or other body parts, by *either* the child or a predator.

Through my discussions with parents, it has been illustrated to me that few parents had told their children to not do the touching and to not allow touching by body parts, including hands.

Understanding grooming methods is of paramount importance for parents in this digital age. However, parents can be groomed too. In so many true cases, parents will say "but we trusted them". The trust is the first component of online grooming, for both child and parent.

One in three girls and one in seven boys will be sexually abused before the age of 18.[12] These are the latest statistics. It is not always older adults. It can be from siblings, friends, friends of parents or siblings, and others.

How do they get there? Parents are so often groomed to trust the predator as well as the children. Who does the grooming? Often, the child does after a predator has instilled trust in them.

If parents question a child about the contacts they have online, the child will adamantly insist the person they have been communicating with, is a true friend. The child may be at the stage where full trust and confidence is with the predator. In these cases, parents have to exercise caution with their child to ensure the situation does not go any further. The child may have already sent nudes, personal information.

It is important to speak to your child about the situation, openly but with calm. The child has already been victimized, even though they may not realize it.

Villainizing them for their actions, will only alienate them even more.

Calm discussion about it is the first step. Ask the child questions – when did it start? How much information has been shared? Have pictures been shared? Were they nudes? Did they receive nudes, pictures, or xxx porn?

- Establish the extent of the situation before going further. Remember, too often, victims have thoughts of self-harm and even suicide, and to discuss it will be painful for them.
- Block all suspected abusers and websites.
- Review the Internet history on the device.
- Gather all evidence you need to help protect your child for their benefit, your benefit, as well as the police if they become involved.
- Remain calm. Your child may resist any help because the predator has them in their grasp.
- Contact police to have the predator traced, if it is possible. Predators need to be stopped, and not by parents. Police will be able to determine the best approach and method. Vigilantes have no place in this type of situation. A predator could be part of an organized crime ring, which

would be more than anyone should attempt to handle.

- Find effective counselling for your child. This type of experience can be traumatic, especially because the child was trained to trust the predator.

Explain to children how pictures can be taken and with what types of devices. Listed below are common ways for predators to take pictures:

- Webcam
- iPad
- Cell phone
- Pen camera
- Eye glasses camera
- WiFi Nanny cam – these devices are used to monitor the activities of a child or infant. If connected to WiFi, the views of the camera can be hacked and a predator record the child and parents. Some parents have had the unnerving experience of having someone speaking to them while they are with their child, through the Nanny cam. If using a type of Nanny cam, choose an offline type of device.

- Dashcam - Police have described dashcams as being dangerous. Some predators have dashcams in the front and back of a vehicle in order to tape children as they violate them in a vehicle. As part of Digital Supervision, parents should be aware of devices in vehicles of people who may be transporting their children.

CHAPTER 12

DETAILS ABOUT CELL PHONES

Cell phones cause risk and vulnerabilities for children more than any other device. According to Eric Schmidt, Google's executive Chairman, there are only two states for children: asleep or online. Being on devices to this extent can cause vulnerabilities because of the length of times children are on them; and, exposure to data and other users.

Researchers are realizing that many young people are vulnerable because of low self-esteem, unsupervised time on devices, little or no adult supervision/support, and perhaps being involved in drugs or alcohol. Older peers are a cause of this because being involved online becomes easier than being offline.

The new "three R's" of literacy – Review, Reputations, Resiliency:

understanding the Internet and Review all activity of children;

management of children will help to guide their digital Reputations;

and with Digital Supervision and constant communication with children, we will build Resiliency for them as they try to cope with the challenge of online communications.

Without adult intervention, children are left to their own devices and most often, lack the life skills to do so. They are lost sheep in the digital world.

For children, the cell phone contains their communications, social media, texting, sexting, data – everything they can use on a computer, laptop, iPad, notebook. The most difficult issue with cell phones? Mobility and lack of concrete supervision.

When I am speaking, I ask parents if they review the content of their child's cell phone on a regular basis. The icons on the phone could be linking to sextortion or sexting rings, and other issues.

Seriously, if you ever drive by an elementary school in the morning or at the end of the school day, you could lose your breath with the smell of exhaust fumes, and children could be killed by a car with anxious parents driving their children to school. They are worried about predators and child safety; yet, they never review anything their child is doing online. It always amazes me that parents believe reviewing the activity of their children online (through computer, cell phone or other device) is an invasion of their privacy. Whatever they do online is public. Their pictures may circulate the world. Online digital use is not the same as a private diary with secrets written in a book. Secrets are no longer "secrets" when shared online.

When land lines were used, parents always knew with whom their child was speaking. They would try to mould their child and ask them not to communicate with certain children or families. Now, few parents actually check the cell phone histories of their children. They are paying the bill and need to know what is going on in their child's life.

To emphasize again, whatever is on a device a parent purchases and for which they have a contract, that parent is responsible for the content. In meetings with police, they have shared they have had to deal with children as young as eight years of age who have produced and distributed child pornography.

Adults in these situations may be interviewed by law enforcement. Questions will be asked regarding how the pictures got there, and what safety guidelines have been practiced by the adults to ensure the children have been protected. In such interviews, the adults who own the devices are interviewed as a possible predator. This is a conversation no caring parent wants to face with police or other members of law enforcement.

Picture this situation – an eight-year-old child with behaviour issues takes a picture of their genitalia and emails it to their friend down the street. The friend's father sees the email and calls police. The police come to your door and proceed to ask you where the picture was taken. You respond with "wow, don't have a clue".

They then interview your behavioural child. When asked who took the picture, the behavioural child says "my father". A child who has behaviour issues never wants to be in trouble. You are then being interviewed as a predator. This conversation is something that could be avoided if parents were practicing Digital Supervision.

Burner cell phones are items for which parents and caregivers have to be alert. Burner phones are prepaid mobile phones that can be replaced frequently. They provide temporary phone numbers that are disposable. They can be used for online ads, travel, business projects or dating. They are also used for illegal transactions such as drug dealing or illegal arms sales. They can be used by youth to substitute a phone their parents have withheld, or to have an extra phone for activities they do not want their parents to know about.

Youth are using them in order to engage in activity outside of the knowledge of the parents. They use them when their regular phones are taken away or if they want to purchase drugs, do things their parents would disapprove of, and other activities. Even if the cell phone lacks a data plan, *any phone can access the Internet through Wi-Fi.*

When parents decide to take away cell phones for one reason or another, teens can feel anxious, lonely or upset. They feel alienated from their cellular community. Principals have reported that in just about every high school, there is someone who sells burner phones from their locker or other location.

A report from the Associated Press stated that many youths are living lives online that their parents know nothing about. There are ways for parents to monitor the activity, but an unknown burner phone is another issue.

One set of parents took the cell phone away from their daughter. They were amazed when she didn't put up a fuss. They realized later that she had obtained a burner phone and was still able to conduct her online communications in spite of the withdrawal of the cell phone privilege at home. Burner phones can access the Internet through free Wi-Fi, and children find those locations. They can also use the family Wi-Fi if the password for the router is known.

To keep devices organized within a home, all IP addresses should be recorded for all devices. The parents or homeowner can access the router to review IP numbers for devices to investigate if an additional device is using the gateway to the Internet of the home. If another device is detected, it could be a burner phone of a child if the regular phone has had the privilege removed.

When parents have given a cell phone to a child, it is important to supervise use. One way is to install a _comprehensive keylogger_ on the phone. The keylogger will record all key strokes as well as any pictures taken using the device, or received by the device. It is still important to review the cell phone, with or without the knowledge of the child. Sharing that there is a keylogger on the phone is something parents can choose to do or not.

With a keylogger, a file can be sent to the parent every day or however often is required. The file would be sent to the parental iCloud account or other location and can be reviewed nightly. It will tell parents about all communications, if their child is a victim or bully, or if there is a predator grooming their child, pictures their child is sending or receiving, and other details. Are children able to work around a keylogger? They might try to delete it; however, a parent will know if it is deleted because they will no longer receive the file for review on a daily basis.

There are software filters available for cell phones. Unfortunately, too often the software filters can be bypassed by the child. Filters will provide daily reports to parents as well. However, the keylogger will provide greater detail and a simple method of supervision of the device.

As stated in the play narration, parents can also mirror the cell phone of their child. There are several app choices that provide this option. The phone of the parent would require installation of the app, with direction given to the cell phone of the child. Activity will then be sent or "mirrored" to the parent.

In addition to using apps, parents should have a contract for behaviour and use of the cell phone (and other digital devices) with the child. The contract needs to outline parental rules: the device should not be taken to bedrooms or bathrooms, no nudes, no unknowns for friends, no personal information, no sharing of cellphone, and more. Sharing of cellphones must be avoided because some youth will use shared cellphones to conduct criminal activity. It is up to parents to establish the guidelines but a contract gives the opportunity to have the open communication necessary to organize digital device use.

In addition to mirroring, key logger, and others, parents must keep communication open, and with a contract for rules, withdraw the phone if rules are broken. The contract must outline consequences. The communications and discussions about technology are important – the children must conduct themselves according to expectations in any type of situation or environment, and in a friend's home. Consistency with parental expectations is key to having children safe.

CHAPTER 13

SECURITY AND TRAINING CHILDREN

It is important to have a computer filter used in combination with Digital Supervision. A filter and Digital Supervision should be considered interdependent for child and family online safety.

There are different types of filters - hardware and software. To define them generally and without specific manufacturing labels:

One type of filter is a software filter. It is installed on a device and manipulates data to ensure only certain data is brought into the device.

There are different types of software filters that block certain websites to ensure children do not view inappropriate websites. These types of software provide parental controls beyond the basic controls provided through the OS of the machine.

There are other types of software that can be purchased to provide increased parental controls.

Regardless of the software used for parental controls, parents have to realize such environments have _limitations_. They are advised for younger children but as children mature, they learn methods to bypass the blocking software while on the Internet. It is also difficult when children are gaming online, even though they are using the router and Wi-Fi to connect to games, because through a gaming system, they are using the server of the game, and outside the computer parent control software.

Parents can set parental controls on gaming systems. Each system is different and it is important for parents to learn the gaming system and set controls as necessary. It is also important to check the history of gaming and make sure a child is not on games that are undesirable for their age group.

Hardware filters are devices that are installed between the router and the computer. They are designed to manipulate data and filter out websites that are inappropriate as well.

Again, Digital Supervision must be practiced in every household. Technology alone will not provide enough supervision for children.

This generation is the most independent generation in the history of the world. Too often, their independence is causing alienation of the children from the parents, which is can be causing loneliness and anxiety.

As stated earlier, over 20% of adults and 80% of children stumble upon xxx pornographic sites "by chance". In other words, they are simply performing queries in general, or on specific sites (YouTube), and find the material in error. This is what I refer to as "collateral damage" for children. Children viewing videos and having a xxx porn video listed as a choice with a child's type of video, is becoming too common.

At issue as well, often organizations and police may issue lists of websites and apps that parents should monitor for the safety of their children. It is excellent to be aware of these sites, however, it can give a false sense of safety. Why? Predators are everywhere. Parents who choose to monitor regardless of environment, are making the best choice.

This is no different than pre-digital choices. Before the digital age, parents gave children choices and parameters regarding their relationships. Parents would have rules that children followed when their parents were firm in their communications. They would follow the rules no matter where they were, and without their parents present.

What happens when Digital Supervision is being practiced in a home and a child goes to another house to play? It is erroneous to assume that children will make the right choices no matter where they are, depending on the rules and communications with parents or caregivers.

In such situations, it is best that the communications have been explained by parents with adequate detail so that children will realize the necessity of making the correct choices, for their own benefit and safety. When given adequate communications and rules by parents, a child will make the appropriate choices when in situations and/or homes that do not follow Digital Supervision and the guidance they have experienced in their own homes. The child or youth will take ownership and make the choices they have been trained to make by their parents. It should be considered the same as whether a child could go into a store and engage in shoplifting. What are the consequences of such behaviour and will they make the choice their parents have trained them to do?

If a child is at a friend's house, and all children are engaging in self exploitive activity, the child who has had Digital Supervision, should choose to leave and make the right choice.

Children and youth also need to be aware that if they engage in inappropriate behaviour and may be charged, they could end up with a criminal record. This changes things for the child/youth and the entire family. For example, if the family wants to go to Disney World, Europe, or another trip, the child who has made a mistake will not be able to travel. They cannot leave the country if they have a criminal record. This changes for the child as well. It will influence careers, and other liberties they take for granted.

Social media cites are reviewed by police. As a network administrator, I had police in the school asking to review certain students, and the headers on their emails. Students were arrested for going against a "do not associate order", and other court orders.

A digital journey must be considered by everyone. Have you left a digital history that will implicate you or your family? Your path is traceable – it is only a matter of time.

CHAPTER 14

EMAILS AND METADATA

"Stranger danger" has a whole new meaning online. With whom is your child chatting? Do you know? Do they know? There are so many ways for a stranger (or a known) to disguise their identity and have a child or youth do what they want them to do. It is not just meeting someone in a park. That is the less sophisticated predator action.

Too often, predators want to have nudes of the child. Readers have to realize this is any child at any age – from birth to 18.

This can begin as a chat during a game. The child or youth will go into a private chat environment. Then the real grooming will begin. They want a picture of the child. They exchange pictures. The predator usually will not send an actual picture of themselves – it will be someone else. Then the child begins to send the inappropriate pictures.

So, you have told your children not to game or chat with strangers online. You told them not to send pictures through the gaming system or chat rooms. Now, your child has created a new email account – Hotmail and Gmail are very easy accounts to create.

The child takes a nude of themselves and decides to send it to the predator. The geolocator on their phone is live. What is a geolocator? It is a part of the operating system that will give the coordinates of exactly where a picture is taken, or where a person is who is gaming with another person. It can be so accurate that the longitude and latitude (a geotag) of the location could even be so accurate as to provide the possible location of the room in a house in which a person has taken a picture or is gaming. On a picture, the location information is included in what is referred to as the "meta data" of the picture.

So, your child decides to send a picture to the predator via email. The picture has the meta data included in the data for the picture (automatic if geolocator is turned on). The predator will have two different pieces of information regarding the location of the child. The meta data for the picture and the header of the email. The header contains information regarding the location of the server from which the email was sent, including the IP address of the machine used to send the email.

A predator, if they want to know more about the child, will use the meta data and the header of the email to locate exactly where a child is living. Sending an email with a picture attachment is not a safe thing to do if communicating with an unknown.

For example, a mother had a pool party for her six-year-old son, with many of his friends in attendance. She took many pictures and put them all up on social media.

Three weeks later, the police came to her door and asked if the picture in their hand was a picture of her son. She was terrified. A person had morphed the picture of her son in a sexual position with a predator. She was being interviewed as a possible suspect. However, the police were suspicious the picture had been obtained via social media and absolved the mother of any wrong doing.

How did they know the location where the picture was taken? The picture had meta data on it with the geolocation included. In recent years, a number of social media sites have made it a practice to strip the meta data off pictures when they are uploaded. However, some photographers want the meta data left on because of their copyright protection. Will they include meta data again? Maybe.

Too often, parents "picture bomb" social media with pictures of their children. It seems to be an inherent competitive instinct among parents. Their friends have put multiple pictures of their children online. Does that make them less of a parent? Does it seem they are not proud of their children? My advice to everyone is to share pictures of their children with family and friends who truly care, the "old-fashioned" way through email, without broadcasting the pictures in a platform that can be public, depending on the settings of the owner of the social media account.

Too often children and adults will send an email to a recipient thinking they cannot be traced – a choice being used rather than social media.

ANYTHING is traceable on the Internet in some way. The safest choice is to only transmit information to trusted recipients, and even then, you cannot be too sure.

CHAPTER 15

PORNOGRAPHY - PREPARE OR REPAIR?

As stated earlier, our children are being exposed to xxx pornography and most parents are unaware. The exposure of children to this type of material is far greater than adults who are surfing the Internet and not looking for it. Why? Predators use pornography for grooming children.

As part of Digital Supervision, parents need to have the realization their children will probably be exposed to xxx pornography. Pornography is considered a major public health crisis in most countries. Digital Supervision equips parents to prepare their children for the possibility of the accidental viewing of pornography, and to repair the damage of such a viewing. The biggest part of it is open communication with children – always.

The viewing of pornography can change the sexual functioning and development for children, both male and female. Why should parents be talking to children about it? Pornography can be as addictive as alcohol, drugs, and other addictions. The police have told me children as young as six can be addicted to pornography.

Some parents have said "oh but it is healthy to be curious about sex for children". There is a difference between a healthy curiosity about their bodies and viewing xxx pornography. There is a minimum age limit on that type of material for a reason – usually 18.

This issue is also becoming a problem for child custody battles. I have received phone calls from one parent in a separation situation, saying their other parent allows full access to anything on the Internet without supervision. In fact, this parent's lawyer had written into the separation agreement, the other parent must practice the Theory of Digital Supervision.

At what age should a discussion take place with a child? This varies based on the child and the parents. My first suggestion is to keep children off line as much as possible. If a child is permitted to be online, my suggestion is age ten and up. Children will learn the Internet early enough in life.

Having ability online and on a computer, does not necessarily mean a child is a genius. Too many parents become excited because a child is creating things and playing online with ease. I have taught many children with intellectual challenges who were extremely efficient online and with gaming.

It is important as a parent to be calm, open, and communicate with children about all subjects. With love and caring, these communications can be productive and positive. Children should not feel intimidated discussing seeing pornography. Once the communications are open, children feel comfortable, it is important to set boundaries and rules related to inappropriate material online. These rules need to be enforced so that the child will make the right choices online, and will make the right choices when at a friend's house.

This is where the old ways of going to a friend's house must prevail. Different rules and leniencies have always existed in various homes. A child needs to realize consequences and make the right choices whether parents are present or not.

Parents/guardians should consider that their online behaviour will set an example for children. If parents are viewing pornography, children will learn the example. Further, if parents are viewing pornography, the chances of children "stumbling" on the material are far greater because of browser histories and data on the hard drive of the machine, if it is shared throughout the family.

Defining pornography may be difficult for some parents. It is important to discuss nudity and what is appropriate. Discuss pornography and children viewing it. Detail is not necessary but the fact a child should discuss it with a parent is important.

If a child needs even more detail, it should be described as grownups without clothes covering their private parts and in positions that are close to each other. Every family is different – the discussion should be comfortable. Some families might want to consult a therapist as to the best approach on this topic.

Preparation as described is extremely important in this digital age. How do you repair the damage after a child has been exposed to pornography?

The reaction of the parents is important. At certain ages, children have a naivety that does not give them a curiosity to search pornography. They have discovered it by accident.

On some websites, predators will insert pornographic material to prepare a child for grooming.

Parents need to remain calm and have an objective conversation with the child. Ask the child what happened and how. What did they see? Share with the child that they are too young to understand what they have seen.

When I speak to children aged 10 to 14, I tell them to talk to a trusted adult – parent, religious leader, teacher – about what they have seen. Viewing this type of material will cause anxiety for the children (they don't want to be in trouble and instinct tells them they could be disciplined for what they have seen), depression, loneliness, and other emotions.

Through my experiences, it is also important to ask the child if someone has shown them this type of material or, has a child at school told them about it and how to go on the websites. This opens up a whole new issue. Who could have guided them to such a site if it wasn't accidental? If it was an adult, it becomes a new discussion. If it was another child, it becomes an issue for the parents of the other child, are they in an environment that allows this type of material, and more. Each situation is different and has to be dealt with through the specific circumstances discovered.

After it has been discovered a child has viewed pornography, it is important to discuss the negative aspects of it but also to outline rules within a household that must be followed. Parents should be reviewing browser histories, pictures on cell phones, and other devices. Tell the child to openly share if there is another issue related to pornography for which they are exposed.

If a child has a pornography exposure, I always suggest professional assistance, as with any possible addiction. I have talked to families that are facing, or have faced, this challenge. It is important to have open communication and rules of engagement with the child but professional intervention early. Every situation is different. To give specific advice in this type of situation could be damaging. The uniqueness of challenges requires professional, therapeutic assistance from a professional who has experience and is trained in this area.

Addiction to pornography can happen at any age. The neuroplasticity of the brain is affected and causes a compulsion to continue to view it. Neuroplasticity is at its highest for children as they grow. Because of this, what they learn viewing pornography will have a life-long impact as they mature. The greatest risk is learned sexual behaviours and attitudes. This can cause objectification of females and sex, and poor sexual behaviours early in life.

A child can be exposed to pornography through social media, emails, gaming (other players/predators will send it as part of grooming), cellphone, computer, laptop, iPad, sexting – just about anywhere with a plugin.

Another question to ask a child is if they have seen a printed copy of pornography. This conversation would develop around a known adult who may have shared inappropriate material with the child, which opens a new issue. Any adult who is intentionally sharing pornography with a child should be considered as grooming the child and has no good reason to do so.

CHAPTER 16

TRUE CASES

True story – some male teens outside of Montreal decided to convince their girlfriends to pose in erotic positions. They told the girls they were using SnapChat and that the pictures would disappear. The girls laughed and decided to go along with the idea.

Unfortunately, the boys used screen capture and shared the pictures through a sexting ring they had developed. All teens were charged with producing and distributing. This is most unfortunate for their futures.

In some cases, children and youth have disguised the location of inappropriate pictures through what would appear to be a benign icon on the screen of the phone or other digital device. In one case, they used the icon of a calculator. In another, the icon of the globe of the world. In any case, they made it so that their parents or adult ally would not realize the real reason for the icon.

In the case of the teens above, they were sharing the pictures in multiple locations and countries through a sexting ring they had developed.

A girl in the United States decided to share a nude of her chest with her boyfriend in high school. Of course, the picture began circulating in the school. She became very distraught, a type of situation that is causing extreme anxiety, depression, and feelings of suicide in many schools and environments involving youth. This girl, at the age of 17, was put on the sex offender registry, and will be on it for life. Her life is basically in a shambles, to say the least. Being put on the sex registry is common in some countries with this type of criminal charge.

I had a father ask to be a volunteer for my charity. He was a survivor of child pornography and had a determined focus to help victims. Upon my second meeting with him, he told me he probably could not be a volunteer. His 17-year-old daughter was being charged with producing and distributing child pornography. He was devastated.

The daughter had been at a party and taken pictures of friends of hers being intimate and practically nude. The friends were under the age of 18. She made the poor decision to post the pictures on Facebook. She broke many laws – she produced the pictures, distributed them, and was in possession. The other issue under Canadian law – it is illegal to share an intimate picture without the consent of the person or persons in the picture.

Children and youth believe such behaviour is comedy and lacks consequences. When speaking to children/youth, it is explained that the laws in most countries dictate that these types of exploitive activities are not comedy but criminal behaviour. Their parents could be "in trouble" with the police. After explaining it, children become subdued.

The seriousness of these types of choices cannot be explained enough. I have often said, children rarely listen to their parents (what do they know), their teachers (they can be defiant with teachers), or the police (they are usually fearful of the police).

After I speak with a group of children or youth, there is an understanding. They realize I have had experience and have knowledge about the truths related to their everyday challenges. As so many people have said, they cannot believe my determination! I laugh and say "you have to live it to understand it."

CHAPTER 17

REAL-LIFE INTERVIEWS

The following chapters introduce the reader to real-life situations through interviews with people who have worked in the field of Internet child exploitation, been a survivor of child sexual abuse, and a survivor of child pornography. The professionals were also interviewed for a documentary series for which I was the Producer and Host.

The first interview is very compelling, with a child pornography survivor; and, an interview with his wife. They have four children. The interview experience with them was emotional for me, but both husband and wife wanted to share their stories, hoping to contribute to the proactive safety of children worldwide.

Susequent interviews are with a criminal lawyer who has defended child pornography criminals. His story opened my eyes to the "other side" of the crime. I am not sympathetic to predators, however, the lawyer did explain how the process occurs.

The police officer who had experienced dealing with cases of child pornography added enlightenment regarding the police handling of the crime, and application of the criminal code.

The psychotherapist who has treated child pornography victims/survivors added an understanding and greater compassion for the life-long struggles of the victims/survivors and their families.

Interviewing a survivor of domestic sexual abuse gave an interesting explanation of this type of abuse, without child pornography pictures.

I am grateful for the transparency and willingness of all participants to want to make a difference for the safety and protection of our children. Sharing their stories gives a reality that is required for improved understanding of the crime and challenges in this digital world.

CHAPTER 18

CHILD PORNOGRAPHY SURVIVOR "PAUL"

In my travels, I meet many people. One day I was leaving my hometown by train on a day trip to Toronto, Canada with my husband. We began chatting with a fellow at the station. He said he had four children and I gave him my business card for the charity, thinking he might be interested in a proactive approach to protecting his four children online. I thought nothing of it and boarded the train.

Within minutes, I received an email from "Paul" telling me his history and that he had been a victim of child sexual abuse and child pornography. I was amazed that the two of us met so 'coincidentally'. He and his family have become good friends and now live close to where we live. We moved and didn't realize they were so close.

His story is compelling and one everyone should read. This type of abuse is happening everywhere, with knowns and unknowns. Paul experienced both. He has grown into a strong man, with some baggage, but a person to be admired.

This is our interview. Thank you so much Paul for sharing. He is hoping children might benefit with more adults knowing the horrific experience child sexual abuse and child pornography have on the victims. There are too many and growing in numbers.

Charlene: Paul, thank you for agreeing to share your story. I know it is a difficult topic for you to discuss. Are you ready and prepared for any triggers you may have throughout this discussion?

Paul: Yes. I am ready. If there are triggers, I will let you know, but I have been able to deal with them better each day. Much more as I age than before. It was extremely difficult prior to treatment.

Charlene: Excellent. Please share a bit of your story so that people will know and understand the magnitude of your experience.

Paul: For starters, I was a victim beginning at a young age until I was eleven years old by a family member.

He took sex pictures for himself and a neighbour. There is more in my history, which I can discuss later.

Charlene: How did the predator groom you to comply? What were the stages if you can remember them?

Paul: I was very young and it was stressed to keep it a secret. If I resisted, he threatened to be violent, overpower me, threatened to kill the baby in my mother's belly. If I didn't fully satisfy his needs, he would threaten to rape my sisters. On several occasions, I was forced to watch him rape my sister (Angela was 3 years younger than me, but severely diminished capacity... my second sister Amanda is 6 years younger than me, and I managed to save her from the assaults). I was also coerced through "soft grooming". I was told there is nothing wrong, it feels good, and I would get rewarded for the activity - either candy or something else. I was given a cigarette as a reward around seven or eight, and marijuana at eight or nine.

Charlene: Were digital pictures used or an instamatic camera or other means of photography or video?

Paul: There were no digital pictures. Instamatic, polaroid and traditional pictures were made. Videos were used as well in VHS or BETA format. I was made to watch as pictures of sex with my sisters were being taken.

Charlene: Please describe your relationships with the offenders. Known or unknown?

Paul: My grandfather and namesake was put in an asylum for 6-9 months and when he got out, he quit drinking and left my grandmother with Billy my uncle still at home with her. She (my grandmother) was raised very poor because her father delivered heating oil by truck, and when she was quite young, five to nine years old, he delivered an entire truck without collecting, pulled on a backroad and piped the exhaust into the cab. Not only did the suicide not have any insurance, but they went after Grandma for the cost of the entire truck of oil. She married "Paul" at around 16, which was normal. She became pregnant, and fairly quickly got pregnant, which quickly developed pregnancy induced high blood pressure, but a team of doctors had a new drug, and told them they could save the pregnancy and the baby. She laid on her back for seven months, not able to put her feet over the side of the bed, or her hands above her shoulders. The baby girl was born alive, about 2 lbs, and lived for a short time... but passed in hours. The doctors told her it was a miracle and a radical success. My mother was born two years later, my aunt about two years after that with my uncle being an accident of antibiotics. I was born shortly after my mother turned 18. My mother didn't touch me for the first six months and we lived with them, until I called Nana "Mama" which would be normal because Nana was so young, and my mother didn't have anything to do with me all that time. We lived with them off and on up to when I turned ten, partly for us, and partly to take care of her and Billy. One night, to prove a point, when I was around seven or eight, my parents were out with my sisters, Nana was sleeping, Billy pulled a pistol, shot it over Nana's bed with her in it, and it drilled a hole in the wall, stuck in Oscar the Grouch's Brick wall. At least all the Guns were removed. Billy was in Martial Arts, and LOVED Bruce Lee movies. He was "Training me to be a "man", teaching me to fight, which was really just him beating me to a pulp.

Charlene: Wow. You have had quite a history. I am sorry to hear this. What other types of abuse were inflicted as a child?

Paul: One day in the backyard, Billy was "teaching" me to deflect or catch knives that were thrown at me. It didn't take long for a blade to stick in my belly. My parents took me to my uncle's place, where his wife was a surgical nurse and she sewed me up. She sewed up slashes on my arms and legs before, and after the stomach incident, I was too scared to have my parents take me to her again, and I only stitched myself up. I have no fear of guns, and was raised with them, but the sight of blades absolutely petrified me. When I moved on my own, I desensitized myself to knives, and collected them and still do. Not kitchen knives, but fighting knives. I got pretty good at using them as a child. Billy "taught" me about sex, oral, masturbation, and I was soddomized regularly "teaching me positions". More than once he had me dig pits, always deeper than my reach, and verbally torture me while digging, and when deep enough he would just start throwing dirt on me to "teach" me how to get out and not get buried alive. The soft grooming was tied to the violence, almost always "teaching" me. In pictures of me in sexual positions, if I didn't perform as he directed, I was beaten regularly. We were watching a Star Trek episode, and the "slaver" had a slave who told Kirk and Spoc "His rewards are lavish, but his punishments are equally as lavish", and Billy revelled in that line and repeated it often enough to stick to memory. Drunken cruelty and drunken abuse. He beat me several times for asking him if he was gay, because of his abuse of me. Being groomed from such a young age I had a target on my back… and I was so hyper sexualized that I stuck out. The people who went out of their way to protect me, I give all prayers of blessings to because they gave me a shred of decency and hope that got built on by some very caring and dedicated people.

Charlene: Did your parents ever find out about the relatives? How did that go?

Paul: Uncle Roy was diminished in capacity but the great grandparents and parents knew the whole time. Billy – everyone knew and they said "boys will be boys". It was ignored, covered up, and kept a secret.

Charlene: Were the police ever involved? I know years ago often this type of thing was ignored because people did not discuss it. In your case?

Paul: The police were involved with my diminished capacity sister, but nothing came of it. Since my father was suspected because he systematically raped his sister, my mother and mother's sister. Which place and what time was not determined and therefore thrown out of the courts.

Charlene: Was there ever a court case for any of your abuse?

Paul: The only case that went to court was for Bud Fisher. Initially, he was charged with sodomy x 2. I believe he was murdered three days before the preliminary hearing. He had been tortured, his genitalia cut off and stuffed down his throat causing lactic acidosis. It is my understanding that victims of his sexual assaults did the dirty deed. I am not sure who but I did not. I was questioned by police and it was determined I had nothing to do with it.

Charlene: Do you have permanent emotional damage?

Paul: I have thought of and attempted suicide at times. I have been diagnosed with Acute Complex PTSD. It has caused many issues for me from physical violence in childhood to psychological and emotional challenges. Anxiety, depression, paranoia, and others. I am also hypervigilant to my surroundings, which are all emotions I try to keep under control to this day. I have had lots of help and years of treatment. My wife and children are great sources of support, love, and understanding.

Charlene; Do you have any permanent physical damage?

Paul: Yes. I have sphincter damage with anal rectal scarring which causes issues. I also have acquired brain injury. This was caused by being hit in the front of the head so many times.

Charlene: How unfortunate. I never thought of the sphincter damage being possible but it makes perfect sense. Terrible. Have you had therapy of any kind? Has it been beneficial?

Paul: I saw a counsellor at the ages of eight to twelve. From twelve on, I received intensive psychotherapy one to five times per week with one to eight hours per session. From fifteen to nineteen years of age, I met with a psychiatrist weekly. I do recommend therapy of any kind is necessary. However, people need to "shop" for a therapist to make sure they are compatible and will understand your situation. Trust and understanding are so important. Without those two components, therapy will be useless. The intensive psychotherapy really changed me and my life, because there was trust and understanding. Sometimes, it has been my experience, if I became a priest and other people were giving a confessional or sharing their issues. It must be the patient talking, not the "professional" sharing and leaning on the victim.

Charlene: What would be your advice to parents as to what signs to watch for if their child might be abused sexually?

Paul: For starters, hypersexuality. If a child is exhibiting these types of behaviours at a young age, it should be reason for concern. Children can go two different ways: one, would be total aversion to any type of touching. If all of a sudden, a child changes and doesn't want any touching after being alone with someone, it is important to calmly ask the child why. Or, if a child is touching in a sexual way that is not typical of their age, this would be cause for concern. The second thing to watch out for, is total embrace. The text book case of many children who have been sexually abused, is to have no regard for their own bodies and act out sexually with anyone. It becomes a sexual fetish.

Charlene: Anything else?

Paul: Yes, I was a victim of child on child sexual assault, which I understand is a problem today with the Internet and children viewing pornography. They don't know what it is all about but experiment. My uncle was just six years older than I was, at the time of his molestation of me.

Charlene: In this digital age, child pornography is shared globally. Too often, victims worry about the pictures and who might be looking at them 'today'. What are your thoughts on this?

Paul: I had child pornography made – pictures and videos. It would be very difficult to think they might be online. To this day, I hate having my picture or a video taken of me. It is very triggering for me. I do remember there being a newsgroup with pics and videos and hoped Bud Fisher videos were not on them. The story had public access. I was in a panic to delete email, and try to hack the newsgroup servers. I tried to break the MIRC thread but couldn't. I was really upset. To have multiple pictures online would be terrible and very stressful. The scariest thing about sexually exploitive pictures online is the integration of "Facial Recognition" where you drop a picture into google search and it brings up all the matching photos. I can only imagine the terror of thinking that a spouse, classmate, teacher, employer, or your children doing a google face search and having sexual assault pictures of you returned. Court anonymity does not exist and anyone doing the search learns of the sexual assault with absolutely no controls. Imagine that Kristen French and Leslie Mahaffey (Canadian snuff film and rape victims) were victimized today instead of the early 90's. Take the newspaper headshot and google search facial recognition and it pulls the snuff films from the deep, sick and twisted part of the web. Everything from revenge porn, slut shaming, self-exploitation - is a huge problem, and with how simple it is, drop a picture of someone in google, and the internet never forgets, and the childhood abuse is right there. No court order for identity can prevent this, nor publication ban, because it is your face, and the technology is only getting better with more matches from more sources. I disagree with adult pornography, but it is legal, but when in an article I read recently a woman who did a couple of pornographic scenes in college years ago, and now she is married, with children and a career, but if you google search her face, the films she is in come up. It

CHARLENE E. DOAK-GEBAUER

makes me think about the strippers who do not have sex for money, I totally disagree with that too because it debases the person, but a google face search and potential boyfriends, landlords, employers.... stage name doesn't matter anymore. For victims of child pornography, multiply that exponentially for the fear, and trauma from the constant revictimization.

Charlene: Did you feel betrayed by your family in any way?

Paul: Yes, absolutely. No one did anything. And when something was realized, I was made to keep it a secret. Parental betrayal around sexual interference is almost impossible to forgive, and even at that, it will never be forgotten. To be made to keep it a secret, only helps the predator. I will say that the system helping men and women who were sexually abused as children still needs a lot of work. People need to understand that boys are victims, not just girls. In fact, there are many boys victimized. Too often, they are ignored because people do not want to believe it. Or, a boy doesn't say anything because he is scared of the consequences of people not thinking boys are victims. It is real. Bud Fisher had multiple victims, and he isn't the only predator with

166

multiple victims who were boys. I want to make very clear, I had nothing to do with the botched robbery and death of Bud Fisher by four young men. In closing, let me emphasize that the system needs to help victims more so they can become survivors. The victims need to be able to assist in transforming the system to a more effective level. With the Internet, there are more victims increasing every day.

Charlene: Thank you Paul. I am sure you will be an inspiration to other victims and parents who are suspicious something has happened to their child. This will help to make a change or to help a victim. And, as a victim myself, I emphasize that it is not your fault as a victim. It has taken me years to come to that conclusion.

Paul: Yes. Take the fault away from yourself and put it where it belongs – on the predator. Also, for your readers, I have had many, many years of therapy and I'm still petrified of becoming my father, or my mother, or even the people in my life who look the other way. I pray for a shred of self-respect, self-confidence in being something positive. I pray that my contribution is more than "not doing anything at all". I understand those people who tried to destroy me for my potential… because I know real darkness, not the shadows that are the absence of light, but the living active darkness. I used to call it dark matter… anti-matter because like there is no such thing as cold, only the absence of heat… shadows are the absence of light, and this darkness is the thickness of oblivion, the ether, and ad as they say, when you look into the pit, sometimes the pit looks back. To their credit, for a time I fully embraced it… the raw power, the chaos, and bliss of destruction. Then I was saved by a young Baptist minister who didn't even have a Church yet, his wife a daughter of a fundamental Baptist, who honestly believed that she need not fear… yeah though I walk through the valley of the shadow of death I shall fear no evil for the Lord is with me. I embraced light and have been fighting ever since. Now I have my wife, you, and a respected member of the clergy to help me.

Paul, Child Pornography Victim Survivor

CHAPTER 19

WIFE OF CHILD PORNOGRAPHY SURVIVOR "PAUL"

Charlene: Welcome K. I am so pleased you are able to be interviewed today. How long have you been married to Paul?

K: Fourteen years.

Charlene: Have you seen changes in his emotional challenges or has he been the same throughout your dating and marriage journey?

K: Definitely, there have been changes. Everything affects him. Because when I met him, he was off the drugs for about a year. Then, they put him on all of the drugs and was heavily sedated. He was probably sleeping 18 to 20 hours per day and they said that was good for him.

Charlene: Is he still sedated on drugs?

K: No, he is not on any drugs now, except pain killers, which is different. Over the years I have managed to get him off the stuff. He believed them for years that it made him a better husband and father. The only way to describe him was that "he was just not there".

Charlene: Has he talked much about his past with you?

K: Yes. From the beginning, he talked to me a lot about it. I was more like a therapist, which helped me to understand him more. I was quite shocked with the challenges he faced and the abuse. It was not normal. What was more shocking to me was that he didn't have the normal childhood most people do. I realized that because of his family history, he couldn't differentiate between normal and abuse. His previous relationships were abusive based on his discussions with me. His discipline from his parents he described as abusive.

Charlene: How was his relationship in his family? I understand there was a lot of abuse when he was younger.

K: Yes, there was a lot of abuse when he was younger. From what I understand, there was a lot of "covering up". At one time, some of his relatives were throwing knives his way. He got injured. His father took him to an aunt who was a surgical nurse. She fixed the injury and sent him home. Other family members knew about it. On top of that, he was sexually abused by an uncle. The family said it was not to be done to girls, but because he was a boy, it was okay. I have been shocked and horrified that this type of abuse happened to him when he was young, family members knew about it, and nothing happened. His great grandparents, and grandparents, could have stopped it. He was dropped off to be babysat with either couple, and his mother did nothing to stop it. They said if you leave him here to be babysat, this is what happens. Paul actually said he thought he was groomed at a young age. His mother's younger brother was allowed to rape him (the uncle was six years older than Paul). No one did anything to stop it.

Charlene: He spoke about Bud Fisher, a realtor from Southwestern Ontario and how he had been taken in by him when he was a runaway at the age of 14. Can you tell me more about this and how you think it affected Paul?

K: Technically, he didn't run away from home, his mother threw him out of the house. He had nowhere to turn. He was walking along the street and Bud Fisher pulled over and offered him a ride. He talked to him about his wife and children and then took him home. There was no one home at the time. He spiked the drinks he gave Paul, that incapacitated him, paralyzed, but conscious. He was paralyzed but knew what was going on. Paul said he was violated that night. The next morning, Bud Fisher repeated the same thing, no drugs, but put a gun on the night stand and threatened him if he didn't comply. After that, he cleaned him up and actually drove him to school. Paul never returned to the Bud Fisher home again.

Charlene: I understand there were other victims. Paul mentioned that Bud Fisher groomed him with child pornography. Do you believe Paul has felt guilt of any kind because of this experience?

K: He actually feels guilt for a lot of things. I don't think he should. It was not like he had a choice as a child – he was small compared to adults. A lot of people even when they grow up, they have submissiveness, but as a child, how much do you understand? He does feel guilty about the other victims that he might have been able to protect from further abuse. He was still just a kid and what could he do? Nothing. I keep telling him that and maybe someday he will feel better about it.

Charlene: How have you felt about it yourself? Does it affect your relationship with him in anyway?

K: No, not at all. We are very bonded. He shares everything with me which makes us closer. I just wish it never happened to him at all. At least when we talk, we have total transparency and understanding. I have shared with Paul that when I was seven years old, my friend and I were playing in a park. A man drove up and had a bunch of coin in the back of his car. He kept sifting through it and asked us to get in the car and help him sort it out. My friend said no, to go. I look back and think that what could have happened? I came close to being abused. Paul has been abused by family members and that Bud Fisher. He has nothing to fall back on. This does cause emotional challenges for him and we always work through those challenges together.

Charlene: I understand you have four children, the oldest from a previous marriage. How might all of this affect them? Or does it?

K: The children are aware of it. He will start talking about it in front of them at times. I send them away and try to play games with them. It is not avoidable because there is really no help out there for him. He has episodes. Sometimes he says he feels suicidal. I tell him to call the crisis line. On one occasion, they wanted him to be hospitalized. The crisis worker called the police. When they arrived, they dragged him into the hallway, handcuffed him, took him to the hospital, locked him into a room without a bathroom, and left him there until a psychiatrist could talk to him. When he talked to the psychiatrist the next morning, the doctor talked to him. He arrived home in a worse condition than he had been before. There are very few people who truly understand mental illness and trauma. There has to be improvement because too many times he has been in "care", and nothing has helped. Understanding and professional guidance needs to be there. Another time he was really bad, was mixing alcohol with medications, and passed out. I called every number I had to get help. They basically told me that unless he is committing suicide, or murdering someone, we don't have help for him. If he is in this type of situation, I was to call 911. When I called the psychiatrist, they said they had to talk to him but I told them he was in no condition to do so. They refused to talk to me. Later that night, he ended up in jail and his doctor's office called me and said they had an emergency appointment for him. I told them he couldn't because he ended up in jail. I got him out through the mental health office and the Chaplain. It is always – they have no beds. He is highly functional.

Charlene: Is it safe to say that being sexually abused and being a victim of child pornography causes a life-long challenge?

K: Absolutely, for sure. Based on Paul's trauma and emotional challenges, I would say yes. It is important that people are aware and help to change the mental health system. When he had psychotherapy that he was forced into by an insurance company, she would see him once per month. They all do the same thing. They all have a medical file, they are supposed to read everyone's file, but on his file there were rules about not talking about certain things. They usually didn't read the file and then they would say they were different. They wouldn't read the file and say they didn't want to be tainted with another doctor's opinion. They would dig and dig with him and try to get more information. The experiences then come to the awareness and it takes me so much time to get him back on track. Unless a patient wants to talk about it, a doctor should not probe.

Charlene: Do the children talk about it?

K: No, they really don't talk much about it. I am afraid that some things that he does when he really doesn't know who he is, etc. they might think it is a normal way to act and it could affect their relationships in the future. I have discussed this with Paul and we try to curb the normalization of this type of behaviour. But on the other hand, my children were exposed to a family that had a boy, who was friends with our oldest. There was an incestuous situation within their home. The older sister was a predator (a victim herself) raping her younger sister and brother. Our two older children are aware of it and understand this sort of thing now. It may be too much information for them but they are aware and it helps them to understand it all better. It makes them more aware of the world – it is not always safe.

Charlene: I understand there were pics and videos of Paul when he was younger (taken by an uncle for a neighbour), and Bud Fisher was supposed to have videos, in other words, child pornography was produced using Paul. How do you feel about there being pictures and videos? They could be digitized and on the Internet right now.

K: I tell him and the kids, and talk about Internet safety. I tell them the predators can activate the camera, record activities, and go with sextortion. If the pictures were taken a long time ago, it would be a shameful situation. Now, there are so many pictures out there it is a drop in the ocean. Don't be worried about it. Don't care about it. The chances of it being traced back to Paul would be slim. However, predators use your personal fear against you to win. If a victim doesn't care, the predator won't win. If you do care, you lose and the predator wins. We keep our children under strict rules when it comes to digital devices. They, through their knowledge and experiences, fully understand the magnitude of what can happen and are very cautious. Sometimes it is good to have experiences that give you reality so that you will make the right choices that will protect your future. Face it, so many parents will say do it "because I said so". I so disagree with that approach. I believe the children need to have explanations and then they will learn about life, and make the right choices. As always, it is best to learn from other people's mistakes and experiences.

Charlene: Thank you so much K. This should give insight for many readers related to being with a surviving victim. You are very understanding. I see you both as bonded and good guidance for the journey of life for your children. Thank you.

K: Thank you.

Wife of Paul, Child Pornography Victim/Survivor

CHAPTER 20

PHIL SQUIRE, CRIMINAL LAWYER AND CITY OF LONDON, ONTARIO CANADA COUNSELLOR

Charlene: Hi Phil. Thank you for being a part of this interview. Just to confirm, you are a Criminal lawyer with experience defending people who have been charged with child pornography crimes.

Phil: Yes, thank you, I have defended people who have been involved in child pornography. It really does change you when becoming aware of the criminal mind. I realize how it affected me, how it affected the person charged and how it affects police officers and anyone involved in dealing with this crime. It really does change you. It is interesting to see how damaging this crime is to everyone involved. It is a pervasive activity.

Charlene: How would you say this type of crime has it affected you?

Phil: It has affected me a great deal. When I begin a case of defense for someone, and they have been charged with child pornography, I will ask them if they want me to watch the pictures they had seen to clarify that it is child pornography, and most insist that it is not necessary. Unfortunately, in one case in court, the Crown Attorney insisted that the child pornography be watched by people in the court room. I was forced to watch it, which was terrible for everyone in the court room. I can tell you that the Judge was not happy because of the effect on everyone, particularly the court clerks. What I saw was draining, I felt terrible, and helpless to some extent. It was like a black hole in my brain and not easy. Very difficult. The victims were very young. I have since learned that people have become desensitized. There is too much availability on the Internet. It can involve people that you would meet every day and whom you think are functioning members of society. There was no need for them to watch it. What I was seeing was awful but I couldn't do anything about it.

Charlene: That would be terrible. How old were the victims in the pictures?

Phil: They were very young. I would say in the vicinity of about ten years old. People have to remember that this isn't sexual, this is assaultive behaviour. It is the type of behaviour that I can't think of anyone who might condone. I was puzzled by this. Why anyone would be interested in this type of material at all. I think that is one of the terrible things about the Internet. The more people see pornography on the Internet, they become desensitized and they want more and worse. That part of it is surprising to me. People that you would meet every day, people who function well in society are watching this type of stuff. My clients get involved, and some are the type of people you would never think would be involved in it.

Charlene: Do you think they are addicted to porn and then go to other areas?

Phil: That's what I have been told. They become addicted. They become desensitized and want more. It is shocking to the families of the perpetrators that their family member is involved in this. They say it is not a part of their family at home. It is a secret.

That is a problem with the Internet. It has only been lately that the police have been able to get into peoples' computers and see what they are watching. The message is important to people – police can get into that. People may think they are alone in their apartment or home and no one can see what they are watching, but the police can. It is another resource that police have to use. It is unfortunate that when the police are looking for people who are watching child pornography, it takes them away from other areas that require policing as well. It is wrong at all levels.

Charlene: I agree. And in my research, I have realized that pedophiles want to be recognized as a "sexual orientation", much the same as the LGBTQ. They want to be referred to as pedosexuals or other term, which I find totally unacceptable. What is your opinion?

Phil: Right, I have heard that as well. I think we have met a point in society, where we have to begin to not accept certain things. People that are involved in child pornography are on one level, and then you get the people who are actually producing it. In fact, there are some cases we are aware of where the parents are actually using their own children. For the people who actually watch child pornography, I have not been able to come to any conclusion as to what made them watch it. What gets them to that point? It is an addiction of a type that is not healthy. It is really going to be tough to deal with it because there is a shaming, you could lose your career. That may be all we can do at this time. They probably require therapy, which is a difficult thing, because people aren't going to access therapy until they are caught. It is doubtful a person would go to their spouse and confess they are addicted to child pornography and require therapy. It isn't going to happen.

Charlene: It is the crime of secrets. And with our most vulnerable sector, our children.

Phil: And that is the difficulty. It is online and there is a separation there from the producer and the person looking at it. It may be created in Asia or Europe but that does not take away the harm to the family.

Charlene: Yes, and the lives of the children are destroyed as well.

Phil: Absolutely, I can't even imagine the child and their emotional health. It must be terrible. I am always going to assume that if they are in an environment that involves child pornography, who is going to help these victimized children? There is no one there. Law enforcement is necessary.

Charlene: What type of sentencing would people get for this type of crime?

Phil: In my experience, at has been jail time. Crown Attorneys are looking for jail time for this type of thing. People always want them to be in jail longer. I can tell you that any period of time spent in jail for anyone involved with this type of crime is horrendous. We have to look at whether it is a deterrent or not. I don't think people looking at child pornography think of the sentence. They are consumed by the need to do this. A longer sentence may not change this. It is getting out of the darkness that may help.

Charlene: Getting back to your comment about people you would never expect to do it, the police have said it is in all walks of life, professions, neighbourhoods - everywhere. You cannot designate.

Phil: Exactly. I have had a client who was a classic loner whose only company has been pornography. Police said when they raided his apartment, it was the dirtiest apartment they had ever raided. I have also had a person who had a really high-level position with a huge responsibility, involved in charity work for children with handicaps. He had a family. It was so bad and consuming, he actually watched the child pornography at work and that is how he got caught. Unbelievable. But the police are right, there is no particular type of person. A person you think is a great person and then is a user.

Charlene: I have to admire you. In the Canadian justice system, every person charged is entitled to a defense, and you are a person that will do that. I think readers need to understand that lawyers are required at both sides of a crime.

Phil: Absolutely, that is correct. It is important because people misconstrue what lawyers do. If the Crown can prove the case against the client, the person will be convicted. In my cases, it was a case of "were they a consumer or a producer". The computer forensics will determine a lot of that. I will tell you, that it is very rarely a case of mistaken identity. Now what can happen, is that the computer may be registered in someone else's name. It may be registered in the wife's name or another member of the family. Then, the police contact the wife about what is on the computer. It then becomes apparent who is truly involved. It is very rare to have total innocence. It is my job that the appropriate charge has been laid, the sentence be appropriate, and that all facts are covered. I will say that anyone that believes judges don't see child pornography as a terrible crime, are mistaken. They should sit in a court room. They never take it lightly.

Charlene: In conclusion, is there any message you would like to send out there to people about this crime?

Phil: I think my message is to tell everyone that has any idea that they are in private in anyway while they watch this material, they are mistaken. There are police whose job is to track these people down. If you are alone in a room, realize you will get caught. If you are in a position where you are addicted or using this material, get some therapy before it gets out of hand. The police are good at what they do. I have asked police officers how they can do this type of work (watching child pornography) and they said they believe it is necessary. The next time you see a police officer, thank them for what they do. Hats off to them. I have watched child pornography for about

15 minutes in the court room and I hope I never have to do it again.

Charlene: I am in the same situation, and I hope I never have to watch it again. Thank you.

Philip Squire
Criminal Lawyer, City Counsellor, London Ontario

CHAPTER 21

JEFF GREY, RETIRED POLICE OFFICER

Charlene: Thank you for coming Jeff. I really appreciate your support and an input in many different types of arrests including child pornography. Is it quite often that the predator is known to the victim?

Jeff: Thank you for having me Charlene. Yes, sometimes it is and sometimes it isn't. The victim may know the predator or a predator has surreptitiously managed to capture the images of a child or person. The parents may be unaware.

Charlene: Have you been involved in cases where there were self-exploitive activities of children? Or younger children?

Jeff: I haven't done a lot of investigations but there have been cases with teenagers and young children.

Charlene: Please explain what self-exploitation is and how it affects a person who is engaging in it?

Jeff: Basically, they expose themselves (take a picture of themselves nude), whether it be on a whim, dare, or just something they want to do. Or, they are simply trying to get themselves involved in a group. They do it to tell a group that they want to belong and be in their group.

Charlene: So, this would be a teenager taking a nude of themselves – a nude selfie.

Jeff: Yes, it is fairly common. The word used is "sexting".

Charlene: Right, and once it is called sexting, it means they have delivered it to a recipient or recipients.

Jeff: That is correct. And then they have a nude of themselves that can be used anywhere.

Charlene: And, if they deliver it and it is a nude of a person under the age of 18, they are in contravention of the Canadian Criminal Code, correct?

Jeff: Yes, that is right. Once they have shared a picture with someone else, it is then distribution and production of child pornography, depending on the age of the person in the picture.

Charlene: So, at that point, they have produced and distributed child pornography. And, a child according to the Canadian Criminal Code is anyone under the age of 18?

Jeff: That is correct.

Charlene: I have spoken in schools and I talk to the students about their self-exploitive activities and they usually find it funny. They think what they are doing is a joke and they're not realizing that when they do it they are contributing to the crime of child pornography.

Jeff: Yes, that is true because right now with the Internet, everyone has it in their hand - everything in their hand is a camera so they don't think of telling the world they are going on a date tonight or they're going away on vacation. Then, they are putting that information on some type of social media. They will take photos of anything that they can and put it out there to show their friend because they are not sure whether they're trying to be popular or that's just the "in" thing to do. I understand Facebook is not so popular for the younger generation. It's more for the older generation to share, but the younger ones get on Twitter, Snapchat, Panda and other platforms.

They have to understand that once the picture has been sent, they may want to pull it back but you can't. There is no way of stopping that circulation and even though Snapchat may eliminate it after a certain time, it is still out there. The recipients will share it, and others share, and the multiple shares makes it impossible to trace and eliminate if someone wants to do that.

Charlene: That is right. And with Snapchat, there have been cases where teens have taken a screen capture and then are able to share the picture from their own device as often as they want to do so. It is then a permanent picture on the originating device.

Jeff: Correct. What the kids do not understand are the legal implications of their actions. As we discussed, the person who takes the picture of themselves can be charged under the criminal code. Yes, they would be charged as a young offender but then they don't understand the consequences of being convicted of that offence. They may not understand that if Mum and Dad want to take the family to Florida, they may not be able to go because they have a conviction on their file. They may not be able to other things. It may affect their employment down the road. Too many kids think that if they are charged under the Young Offenders Act, when they turn 18, their record is swept clean. It is not. It is still there as they continue on in their life.

Charlene: It is important that people know the legal implications of their actions. It is lifelong then.

Jeff: Yes, there is more to it than meets the eye. Their record is a criminal record and will be there for life.

Charlene: I have been speaking in schools and every time, a principal will tell me they have had a student charged with this type of offence – self exploitation interpreted as child pornography. Have you, as a police officer, run into that type of situation?

Jeff: Yes, I have. It is a tough situation. They usually see themselves as a victim. But, again, it depends on how that person has gone about it, or the reason that person shared that image. If their boyfriend is coaxing them to do it, then yes, they are supplying the picture for someone else. There could be mitigating circumstances where there would be no charges.

However, if people just take a nude picture and then send it out, unfortunately, that is a straight violation.

Charlene: We have talked before, and you explained to me that if you see a number of nudes on a cell phone, you would contact CAS (child and family services) to report the situation. Would you please explain your reasons for doing that?

Jeff: Yes. So often, when people hear of that organization being involved, the red flags go up. They are there not to harm the family, but to protect and assist the family. There are great people working within Children and Family Services. As an investigator, I would do my due diligence and have CAS involved. They may already be working with the family or know of them. They at least could get assistance for the family for what they have gone through and will be going through in these types of circumstances.

Charlene: Regarding child pornography cases, predators will "groom" the victim to do what they want them to do. Please elaborate on what grooming is and how it works.

Jeff: There can be grooming, but in some cases, there is no grooming. There are cases where someone will take a picture of a child and put it out there. In this type of case, there is no grooming at all. It's like the old days where parents would take pictures of their children in the bath tub. Is that child pornography? It all depends on the purpose of why that photo was taken. If the photo is shared on the Internet, then that becomes another issue. We are then sharing that photo of the child with other people.

Charlene: Yes, and the Internet can be accused of causing an explosion of that type of behaviour. With grooming, children can be groomed to trust a predator, but I tell listeners, that the whole family can be groomed. Please elaborate on that Jeff.

Jeff: Grooming is a process of gaining the trust of a child. A person could have a child on their knee, kiss them and hug them, making sure the child believes that is okay. They can then begin touching and say "Oh I am sorry, I didn't mean to do that". They could make it a game. Children are trusting of adults. They may get rewards out of it – let's go to the candy store but don't tell anyone what happened in the car.

Charlene: Yes, and the parents don't question anything because they don't believe there is any reason to not trust the family "friend" or relative.

Jeff: Unfortunately, that is true. Anyone associated with the child will be groomed to trust. Example, here is Uncle Johnny, he is helping, taking the child, mentoring the child, or it is a child of a single parent. I am not saying anything about any organization, but it could be a family friend or neighbour. They start buying them clothes, taking them on trips, etc. The parents believe they are doing a great job and their child loves them.

Charlene: I tell audiences that this can happen, and in today's digital world, there is usually a camera involved. Would you agree?

Jeff: Yes, that is often the case.

Charlene: I believe parents should caution their children about what can be a camera and when not to allow a picture. Or, to tell their parents that they believe someone has taken a picture of them without their clothes on. Let's face it, a pen can be a camera.

Jeff: Absolutely, quite often you would have no idea you are being recorded. It can be a pin-hole camera, cell phone, etc. The biggest thing in cars now is a dashcam. Some can have a dashcam at the front and at the back.

Charlene: My goodness, that would be a way for a predator to victimize.

Jeff: Yes, that is correct. Parents are all doing the best that they can but unfortunately there are individuals that will take advantage of a child.

Charlene: What age group would you say is the most at risk for this type of victimization?

Jeff: Any age group.

Charlene: Birth to age 18?

Jeff: Yes, unfortunately, there are people with fetishes out there that can involve any age – even infants, young children, prepubescent to pubescent. It is unfortunate that there are no parameters at all. Gender, age – there are no limits for this type of criminal behaviour.

Charlene: How unfortunate. What would be a final message you can give to parents and teenagers

Jeff: Parents should be aware of what their children are doing. Do not allow the computer or tablet into the bedroom. They have no supervision of what the child is doing. It used to be a parent would have a child watch a video. Now, they are given a tablet. If you do not what they are doing, you have no way to help them. There may be sites that will draw the child in. If the parent knows what is going on, then they have a chance to guide and protect the child. There are sites on the Internet on which the children should never be involved.

Jeff Gray, Retired Police Officer

CHAPTER 22

SARAH LEYES REGISTERED PSYCHOTHERAPIST

REGISTERED CANADIAN ART THERAPIST

Charlene: Welcome Sarah. I am very pleased that you have time to meet with us today. Please confirm your qualifications and experience with readers.

Sarah: Thanks for having me. I am a registered psychotherapist and registered Canadian art therapist. I treat children as young as five up to 18 and I do to treat adults as well.

Charlene: I do know that you have treated child pornography victims. How do you find them when they first come to you?

Sarah: Of course, the families are usually shocked and maybe in a bit of denial that this has happened to their family and to their child and sometimes the younger children especially, are very confused and don't really understand what has happened. The response that they've received from their parents and having to go meet with police officers and therapists, and all these new people, it's just an unfamiliar process for them and hopefully, it doesn't add to the trauma. It is a part of their story of the event that they experienced. I'll just speak from my experience.

Charlene: Statistics show that often the victimization is done by a family member. Have you found this to be the case?

Sarah: It hasn't been very often in my experience but the statistics do show that sometimes that is the case. Also, they may have been a victim from someone outside family.

Charlene: Many parents can feel guilt over their child being victimized. I often tell them that the whole family is groomed by the predator. What are your thoughts on this?

Sarah: Yes. Because the parents feel bad how often they, would be talking to the predator and not know the possible consequences. Parents often feel guilty and blame themselves. In preparing parents for treatment, their feelings of guilt are part of the big picture. I work with them so that they become aware of their role as the child is being treated. They are the ones at home before bedtime soothing fears and worries and answering questions that might come up for the children. This helps in the time for when the child is not in the therapy office. Definitely, parents find that very difficult. This is just a difficult situation and no family ever imagines that they're going to be in the situation.

Certainly, I think everybody believes that this just isn't going to happen to them.

Charlene: I think in today's society, too many people don't want to believe this is as big a problem as it is with the internet causing an explosion of this type of predation. Do you ever talk to the parents about how much they were groomed along with their child?

Sarah: We may not use that language specifically but we do talk about how they can prevent this from happening again and ways that they can monitor their children. When a child is using electronic devices on the computer or the cell phone or the tablet, whatever the case may be, how important it is for the parent to be aware. Parents want to trust their extended family, babysitters, and others. They don't want to believe that their children are at risk when they're on social media or on the computer in their own home. We talk about how to protect children and different things to watch out for.

Charlene: What would be indicators that a parent should be alert to regarding a child's behaviour or other types of clues?

Sarah: I tell parents to do searches of history on the devices. Often, the child is just not being themselves. Behaviour indicators could be:

maybe they're being over compliant;
maybe they are being defiant;
maybe they're having outbursts of anger more than usual;
maybe the child is not being themselves.

In most cases, parents say that they just don't know what is right - they just know that something might be a bit off. Predators give the children directions so that it is all hidden very well for parents. They might not even notice that there's anything different with a child

Charlene: This is a lifelong trauma that the child will be trying to deal with for a long time. What information can you share in this regard?

Sarah: it depends on the situation and victim. Every situation is different but I know through interviews I've done the child pornography victims tend to wonder where their picture is today and who's looking at it right now. That is a specific concern for this population of children who are sexually abused. It happens in a certain place you know they don't have to revisit that actual location they may want to as part of their healing but they don't have to. With a child pornography victim, it is a reality that the pictures could still be on the Internet or on someone's personal computer. It could be re-uploaded on to the Internet for other people to see. In therapy, though, we look at what we can control and what we can't control. How to feel safe, stable and how to soothe and regulate our feelings. We really work on the victim feeling confident, that we can keep ourselves safe.

Charlene: I know you specialize in Art Psychotherapy. Please explain how this works with children.

Sarah: Art is a good outlet for the child. The younger children commit themselves more to Art, which is a natural way for kids to communicate. They let their defenses come down so they're not so scared of an adult person being in the room and talking with them about things that aren't so comfortable to talk about. When we incorporate arts and play you know that it is so much more a natural way and very beneficial for Children. Talking about intense feelings can be difficult for anyone and when we are traumatized, it is so difficult. What lives in the part of our brain that is the five senses – sight, touch, smell, hearing, taste - when we look to treat it sometimes the trauma just doesn't have words attached to it therefore we have to go in with a message. For example, touching clay, and you smelling scented markers, and feeling the pastels. This is a more direct way to be able to express how you feel and what you've experienced and have someone witness this image that you created. It is through the process of doing that there can be healing.

Charlene: I'm wondering if there's a message you could give readers about protecting their children so that perhaps they don't become victims.

Sarah: I think a full message and important message for parents to hear is that the relationship between parent and child, and/or if a child has someone in their life who believes in them and that the child can trust like a coach or a teacher is so important. It is still relationships and those strong connections that can go a really long way to overcoming trauma. Build those connections really strong so the child can always come to you, and know never to fear that they're going to be in trouble if something were to happen. The best protection vehicle we have is good strong communicative relationships.

Sarah Leyes, R, RCAT, B.ED.
Registered Canadian Art Therapist

CHAPTER 23

CHILD SEXUAL ABUSE SURVIVOR

SHEILA STEVENSON

Charlene: What advice would you give a victim hoping to be a survivor?

Sheila: First of all, it was NOT your fault. Now, please let me explain that I was sexually abused by my own father, and my mother blamed me for what he did. I was about five years old the first time. She then physically abused me until I was about 15, and all through my life whenever I was standing near to, or speaking with a man who was not related, her favourite question was "What did you do to entice that man?" That question was always accompanied by a slap or punch. She totally neglected me emotionally, and was still gas-lighting me until I last saw her in 2009. That's when my serious healing journey began.

You did not do those awful things to yourself, no matter where you were, or what you wore, or what you consumed, or who you were with – at any age. You were used by an unscrupulous individual or groups of persons. I feel it is very important for survivors to know that the human brain is not fully cognitively formed until we are in our mid-twenties. The ability of children and youth to make good decisions is not fully formed. Even if you agreed to having 'a few photos taken', or emailed some to an acquaintance or new on-line 'friend', you were incapable of fully understanding the long-range impact, and/or harm, of your decision.

Charlene: I know you were sexually abused but child pornography was not involved. How would you feel if there were pictures circulating on the Internet of your abuse?

Sheila: Truthfully, if I knew about it, I would be horrified. And I would wonder if I could ever hold my head high again in public, or with friends. As far as I know there are no sexually explicit photos of me online. I dissociated when my father first sexually violated me at around age five. Yet, all through my childhood, teen years and into adulthood he constantly made innuendos of his desire to be sexually involved with me again. He loved to put his hands on me, and was always looking me up and down – you know that feeling – when a man is visually undressing you. I felt violated again every time he did that, and he continued doing that up until his eyesight finally failed in his late 70s. While there are always some people who will judge us unfairly, and even cruelly, they need to be ashamed of themselves, not you or me. When I published my own book Let Your Light Shine! Learn how to overcome the effects of childhood abuse, the only person who was offended was my worst perpetrator, my own mother. Given the statistics of people who have experienced sexual abuse, 1 in 3 girls before the age of 18, and 1 in 5 boys in the same age group, we can surmise that possibly 6 million girls and 3.6 million boys here in Canada alone have been harmed. And, please remember that those statistics are formed from individuals who have reported their abuse. Potentially there are millions more who are holding onto their secrets. Holding on to that type of trauma – in reality any type of trauma – is harmful. It is harmful for the victim and both their mental and physical health. It is also harmful to their relationships, and our societies are faced with the real costs of dealing with un-treated trauma in the form of addictions, mental health issues, homelessness, and most sadly, suicide.

Charlene: I know people have said you will never get over the abuse. Do you believe healing, or overcoming the abuse, is possible?!

Sheila: Several times I have heard some sadly uninformed people say that "You'll never get over what happened to you." That hurts my heart because not only are they spreading that lie, but I suspect they are living it as well. Healing is possible. I am proof. Anyone can check online for what is called the ACE Test. (An ACE score is a tally of different types of abuse, neglect, and other hallmarks of a rough childhood.). The rougher your childhood, the higher your score is likely to be and the higher your risk for later health problems. My score is 9, and I have done an incredible amount of healing. It isn't necessarily easy, especially if help is not available until many years later. However, the healing journey is worth all the effort, because it allows us to freely live our lives. Healing lets us BE who we were intended to be, before someone harmed us. All my harmful experiences and expert therapy have formed me into the happy, powerful and productive person I am today. The memories stay with us, but as I have learned we can shrink them from taking up all our head and heart space, down to a single molecule.

Charlene: What else would you add to help a victim understand about having been "groomed" for being victimized for child pornography?

Sheila: When we grow up we often look similar to our childhood selves, however there is never a need to 'own' up to anyone if they ask about pictures they've seen that they believe maybe you. First of all, if there have seen sexually explicit online photos of you it could be a clear indication that they themselves are watching child pornography. RUN from that person. You do not owe them any explanation. But if you feel you need to say something, a simple "No, that's not me", is not a total lie. Why not? Because you are a different person today than you were then. Again, if someone is being pushy about it, RUN!

Charlene: How difficult has it been for you to stop thinking about the abuse? To stop focusing on the victim rather than working toward being a victor?

Sheila: I have heard it said countless times, that we get what we focus on. For too many years I focused on what happened to me, and I was constantly asking myself WHY my parents did those awful things to me. It is now decades later, and I still don't have a satisfying answer to the 'why'. However, when I was able to finally learn to stop referring to myself as a victim, it freed me up to begin healing. You, and I, were only a victim when the awful things were happening to us. Then we became survivors, and through the journey of healing we learn to become VICTORS! Focus on healing. Focus on being good to yourself. Stop focusing on the perpetrators. They would love to believe they are still top-of-mind to you. Let the police do that!

Charlene: Do you believe your experience has helped you relate to victims as a life coach?

Sheila: Not all professionals really understand the harm that sexual abuse can do to a person. They may have studied about it. They may have helped a few people, but that does not mean they are necessarily the right person to help you. As with any other relationship, the healthy ones are the relationships with which we feel most comfortable.

One of the effects of childhood trauma is that we often learn that we have to 'please' others. Children deserve to explore their world, express their ideas, thoughts and feelings, and be supported, nurtured and cherished. If you sense you are being coerced into working with a professional whom you do not feel comfortable with, you have the right to leave, and search again to find someone else you can trust.

Charlene: I understand you work independently but also in cooperation with therapists. What would be the difference between a therapist and a coach? –

Sheila: A professional therapist is someone who will help you to tell your story and begin to come to terms with what you experienced. They are the expert. A professionally certified coach is someone who will help you to move forward into the life of your choosing. You are the expert, and they are your guide. Choose according to what your need is at the time. Whomever you choose to work with, a professional who is 'trauma-informed' would be best. They have a deeper understanding of the harm trauma causes, and will tend to be gentler and more respectful of you. Choose someone who will help you in your journey of healing, and work with you to move forward. I have worked with therapists, and they with me, in order to provide the most beneficial package for a victim.

Charlene: Many people who have experienced trauma, have what are called "flash backs". Is it possible for someone to control the flashbacks and find improved comfort by doing so?

Sheila: There is no clear definition that can help us pick out abusers before they harm us. They operate in secrecy, and they manipulate us into trusting them. They will say all kinds of wonderful things in the beginning to get us to trust them. That is called 'grooming', and they are very good at it. They are most often adults. Remember, as a child your brain is not yet fully formed, and that makes you vulnerable. Abusers use that. Once they show their true colours, the language they use very often changes. They may begin to tell you messages that hurt deeply, and cause you to doubt who you are. My mother constantly told me that I was stupid and ugly and that no one would ever want me. I believed that – for a very long time. I finally found a wonderful therapist, in my early 40s. She helped me get my story out of my head. One day at home afterwards,

I dropped a glass of milk. The glass shattered, and milk splattered all over the kitchen floor. The first thing I said was "Oh, you're so stupid". I instantly became aware that those were words my mother had spoken to me countless times. In that moment I resolved to make a change. At first I said to myself "No, you're not stupid, Sheila". Then I became aware that there were two 'negative' words in what I had just said. I changed the message to "Sheila, you are smart". From then on I became more aware of the messages stuck in my head that came from someone harmful. From then on my life began to change for the better.

Charlene: Many victims believe they are to blame. The predator is skilled in giving this impression. What could you say to help a person "shed the guilt"?

Sheila: DUMP ANY SHAME THAT YOU FEEL OR THAT HAS BEEN IMPOSED ON YOU – Shame is a very heavy load to carry. The feelings of shame that victims carry does not rightfully belong to them. Even young children have an innate sense of what is right and wrong. When something awful is done to them they think 'cause and effect'. In other words, if something bad is being done to them, then they must be bad.

NO! That is simply how a child's brain works. Shame really belongs to the person harming you. Holding onto feelings of shame simply blocks your ability to begin to heal. It is absolutely okay to verbally tell yourself (out loud works best) that you have no reason to feel ashamed for what someone else did to you. Even if you were coerced into doing things you didn't feel good about, remember that you were either forced or had no choice.

Remember, especially at a young age you were physically, and mentally, outweighed. It was not your fault. You are not alone. You deserve to find healing and move forward.

Sheila M. Stevenson, ACC
Professionally Certified Life Coach
Member ICF – International Coach Federation
https://www.SheilaStevensonGroup.com

CHAPTER 24

OVERCOMING TRAUMA HOLISTICALLY

In addition to being a Computer Specialist in Education and a Network Administrator, I am a Registered Holistic Nutritionist.

After experiencing the trauma of losing Jennie, and discovering child pornography on a computer I was repairing, I suffered with depression and anxiety. In addition, I was in a car accident and diagnosed with WAD III whiplash and concussion. My doctor prescribed medications for anxiety and pain. The medications prescribed made me ill. I wondered what I should do as an alternative because I was affected both emotionally and physically. I have allergies to sulphites/sulphates, sodium laurel sulphate, and sulpha, chemicals in many medications.

After shopping in a health food store, I asked the employee what courses she studied to qualify her to be employed. She explained she was a Registered Holistic Nutritionist, and that the courses she studied might help me understand alternative types of care for my condition.

I went home and researched. Within one week, I was enrolled in the course through the Canadian School of Natural Nutrition in Toronto, Canada, and graduated as a Registered Holistic Nutritionist.

My nutrition became organic and without chemicals. I went to a psychotherapist to help sort out the emotional challenges surrounding viewing child pornography on the computer.

I was advised to attend meditation sessions, and learned different techniques. There are different types of meditation to try. It is up to individuals to decide which one is best for them (loving-kindness meditation, body scan or progressive relaxation, mindfulness meditation, breath awareness meditation, Kundalini yoga, zen meditation, transcendental meditation). My best choice has been mindfulness meditation. I learned to apply mindfulness in my day-to-day activities - concentrating on the moment rather than having my thoughts on "hyper-active" mode.

I realized I was dealing with my challenges "holistically". It is important to understand this type of treatment has been effective for me, but might not be the answer for everyone. However, I advise that the information I am sharing would be of benefit for anyone, but in particular, children and adults struggling with anxiety and stress resulting from trauma.

There are many chemicals in foods that must be avoided to maintain a balance emotionally and physically. These chemicals have a negative effect on everyone, particularly people who are struggling emotionally, including children:

1. Refined white sugar granules, powders and syrups; and refined white flour starches. These items are full of chemicals and processed with chemicals. These two refined white carbs can force a release of your brain's serotonin and endorphin, which is what helps you feel good. This is what can cause a person to want to eat more sugar, which causes more chemicals in

the system and then in the brain. When trying to deal with trauma, the imbalance chemically in the body, will provide more challenges emotionally.

2. Wheat, Rye, Oats and Barley. Some people are sensitive or allergic to these grains. If a person is sensitive to these grains, it can cause emotional fluctuations. They can also cause chronic digestion issues, particularly in the bowels – constipation or diarrhea.

3. Certain fats – corn oil, soy oil, canola oil, safflower oil, sunflower oil, peanut oil, sesame oil, wheat-germ oil, cottonseed oil, walnut oil, etc. These oils can also cause interference with mood altering medications. Olive, coconut and palm oil are acceptable, provided there is no sensitivity.

4. Soy can adversely affect the brain and digestion. It can cause issues with mood. Experts say soy can affect production of hormones as well.

5. Synthetic artificial sweeteners (Aspartame). These products can cause issues – headaches, mood swings, indigestion, reactions similar to diabetes. Organic sweetener choices without the calorie intake of sugar are Xyletol and Stevia. Xyletol can be difficult for some people

to digest and should not be used if there is a hard wood allergy. Stevia is good as long as a person is not allergic to the ragweed family of foods.

6. Caffeine can cause chronic emotional challenges such as depression, hyperactivity, mood swings.

7. Colourings, preservatives and other chemical additives. MSG, food colourings (tartrazine), yellow, blue, dyes – all have effect on mood. When trying to combat trauma, they can cause increased issues.

8. Specific toxic additives – BHT (butylated hydroxytolune), BHA (butylated hydroxyanisole), and TBHQ (Tertiary Butylhydroquinone) should all be avoided. These are synthetic, human-made additives, made from coal tar and butane. They are preservatives, used to prolong the shelf life of food. They can also be found in cosmetics (cleansers, makeup, lipstick, sun blocks – many products). They can be blamed for hyperactivity (not good when overcoming trauma), nausea, vomiting, tinnitus, and more.

9. Synthetic sulphites/sulphates. These are indicated as sodium bisulfate and sodium or potassium metabisulfite, sulfur dioxide,

sodium sulfite, potassium sulfite and bisulfate, sulphurous acid. Other names for sulphites in foods in European products: E 220, E 221, E 222, E 223, E 224, E 225, E 226, E 227.

It is important to avoid any foods for which there are sensitivities or allergies. Consumption of foods that can cause physical issues, will affect emotional challenges.

In addition to making better food choices, it is important to engage a therapist. People should "shop" for a therapist the same way they would for any service provider. Compatibility is important. If a person leaves a therapy appointment and believes it is not working for them, find another therapist.

The holistic approach to nutrition should be seen as interdependent with a good therapist. Both will bring a person closer to recovery than just one choice. This is an introduction to a holistic approach to trauma. Does it work for everyone? Of course not. Some trauma victims require medications, which should not be viewed negatively.

An integrative approach is acceptable. Integrative is defined as including traditional medical approaches (with prescription medications), combined with holistic methods. Be careful if using organic supplements. Medications and supplements can interact, which can cause health issues and cancel prescription medication effectiveness. Any time prescription medication is used, a physician should be made aware of all supplements being used.

Avoidance of chemicals and preservatives in foods should be practiced with any approach to trauma.

CHAPTER 25

WHY DIGITAL SUPERVISION?

So many times, people have asked me why I started my charity, Internet Sense First | Premier Sens Internet (originally called "Child Pornography Hurts"). The ensuing story will explain how it got started, my family struggles, and my personal struggles that led me on this journey.

I will never regret doing something that was begun to help my twin sister, her family, and the entire family. Names have been changed to protect the innocent. I tell very little about my experiences when I am speaking, for the protection of my family and for people to realize – it is all about the protection of children, _not about me_.

There are many situations involving the victimization of children using computer, digital devices, and the

Internet. Unless a person is a victim, or a predator has victimized a family, the effect of these crimes is difficult to comprehend. The general population believes that these crimes are horrid. They have little understanding of the magnitude of the proliferation of the crime and its effects. The story about Jennie and her family in the ensuing pages will introduce readers to the magnitude of the effects of being victimized by digital crime. Jennie was only four when the crime against her and her family took them all into a nightmarish journey of horror. Names have been changed to protect the innocent.

Since the 1990's, the digital age has matured and digital crime has become more prevalent. Parents, caregivers, and professionals need to comprehend the magnitude of the need to practice Digital Supervision for all children on all devices. Children, as young as four, are playing online games and being victimized by child predators who, while pretending to be a child, enjoy playing the games with the children, hiding behind a mask of anonymity.

This family story emphasizes the type of abuse that can be perpetrated by a predator who runs a for-profit or not-for-profit child pornography business using digital devices. Too often, the predator is a person the child has been assured can be trusted, and, unfortunately, a person the parents were groomed to trust. Always be alert to anyone who could potentially be a predator. A predator could be one or both parents, grandparents, aunt, uncle, family, friends, babysitters, unknowns, and on it goes.

Digital still and movie cameras were used in this crime, as well as computer equipment. The data was circulated via the Internet and regular mail. This is a true story.

"Hey Mom!! Guess what? Nancy's Mom says I am so beautiful I should be in movies! She takes my picture and says my colouring is amazing for pictures! This is so neat Mom. I am so happy!".

"Awe, sweetheart. I am so happy you have a new friend in Nancy. Her Mom and family seem so nice. I know you are beautiful!", says Jennie's Mom.

Jennie was so excited and so was Elaine, her mother. Jennie had been quite lonely and lacked friends in their previous neighbourhood. She was all dressed up in her Mary Jane black shoes, lace ankle socks, blue velvet dress, with lace around the collar. Elaine wondered why she was so dressed up to play.

"Jennie, did you and Nancy both get dressed up to play today? It seems so unusual for you to get dressed up! You look so wonderful", said Elaine. She liked Nancy and her family and thought it excellent that Jennie could play at their house.

Jennie was so excited. She said "Nancy's Mom asked me if I could get dressed up today for dress up day. We had fun posing and pretending. It was such a fun day with my new friends!".

Elaine was fatigued from moving. Their old neighbourhood had no friends for Jennie. It was such a relief to have her happy. Doug, Jennie's father, had built their new house. It was open concept with a large lot. The whole family, including all four children, were very happy in their new location.

Jennie was four years of age, and was the third child of four in the family. She always struggled to have friends. It seemed wherever the family lived, there were very few children her age. Her older siblings were five years older and, at her age of four, her two-year-old brother was just developing and not quite her level of maturity to be a play mate yet.

Jennie had begun to play with Nancy just about every day. They lived right across the street. The house could be seen from their house, which made it convenient for Elaine and Doug to keep an eye on Jennie as she ran back and forth to Nancy's house. Elaine would call to have Jennie return home, and it might take about 30 minutes before she would make it home. Elaine and Doug thought nothing of it because they knew Jennie was finally happy. She would come bouncing in from playing with a big grin every time.

After about three months, Jennie started changing her behaviours. They were very subtle at first. She didn't seem so happy when she came home. They asked her if there was anything wrong, and she would shrug her shoulders. She often went into her bedroom and would close the door. This became quite a concern to them. She seemed to be unhappier than in the other neighbourhood. Her communications were very limited with them.

Jennie started making comments about Nancy's mother. She said she was a really good mother and did things with her and Nancy that were more fun than at her house. They played games, watched movies, and had more fun than Jennie had with her siblings.

Elaine and Doug were getting even more upset as time progressed. They could not understand what was making Jennie so difficult. She was also having conversations within the family that had too much maturity for her age. She described a stick she played with at Nancy's house that looked like the head of a dog. All of the grownups played with them using the stick.

Wow. Elaine wondered what the stick could be and began thinking the worst. She spoke to Doug about it, and he began to wonder himself. They were constantly worried about Jennie. She seemed to have the worst luck at times. They certainly didn't want her to be without friends and decided to try to find out what might be taking place.

The next day, Elaine decided to call and have Jennie return home sooner than usual. Nancy's mother said "soon". Elaine insisted that Nancy return home immediately. It took another 15 minutes for Nancy to come home. She had an indignant and angry air about her which really concerned Elaine. She was used to her bouncing home and being happy.

Elaine told Doug about it. He didn't seem too concerned. She told her sister Beth about it and the concerns she had. Elaine was finding Jennie's behaviour unusual, with questions of a sexual nature that seemed beyond her years. Beth told her it was good she was alert to it but to be very careful with what is going on with Jennie. Her last statement was "be mindful and careful. You never know with people."

One day, Jennie was outside with her older sister, Judy. They were laughing and giggling. Jennie would jump over Judy and Judy would try to catch her. It was difficult to understand which one was winning.

Elaine and Doug were thrilled to hear that Jennie was playing so nicely with her siblings. Their hearts ached for her because she just didn't seem to fit in at times. It started after they had moved into the neighbourhood, but they still couldn't put their finger on what might be the trigger.

All of a sudden, Jennie stopped laughing, and yelled at Judy "Show me your privates." She started dancing around Judy yelling "Show me your privates, show me your privates, show me your privates! Right now!". Judy stopped and just stared at Jennie in shock. Judy went running into the house to tell her parents.

They were absolutely horrified. Elaine thought with dread, that maybe she had been right all along about poor Jennie. Both Elaine and Doug spoke to Jennie about her behaviour and asked her why she said what she did to Judy.

Jennie got very angry and went running upstairs. Doug and Elaine looked at each other in bewilderment. Elaine went running upstairs after Jennie. When she arrived at the door of Jennie's bedroom, she saw Jennie sitting in the dark, looking out the window toward Nancy's house. Jennie said, "I wish Nancy's mother was mine – she lets us do whatever we want. She doesn't work either."

Elaine was devastated. She worked as did many of the mothers in the neighborhood. She knew things were not right when Jennie went to Nancy's, and on top of all of that, Nancy's mother was manipulating Jennie into an opinion that was totally unfair. She assured Jennie that her mother and father loved her dearly and that whether they work or not, doesn't change that. Their house has rules and talking to her sister like that was wrong. When asked where she got the idea, Jennie just continued to stare across the street and said "nowhere". Elaine left the room and knew the conversation was going no further.

Doug and Elaine were becoming even more concerned about Jennie. Things were changing with her on a daily basis and they were getting more and more frustrated.

The next day, their sitter, Verna, called Elaine at work. "Elaine, you need to come home now. Jennie is talking about things that are just wrong. The girls are playing in ways that seem sexual. I think things are happening in the house across the street that aren't right. I have sent Nancy home. I am sorry but I just feel it."

Elaine told her boss she had an emergency, got in her car, and could hardly get home fast enough. They lived in the country and the trip seemed as though it took three hours and not the thirty minutes it usually takes. She ran into the house and the sitter was sitting in the kitchen, waiting for her. Jennie was in the living room watching cartoons on TV.

The sitter explained it was the type of play and chatter that caused concern. She was quite pleased to send Nancy home. The girls had been playing quietly and talking about the stick game again, and whom they would be playing the game with the next day. They said that Nancy's grandfather would be visiting and they could play the stick "game" with him too (predators often refer to their twisted activity as a game or play to the victim as a part of grooming).

The sitter, again, had asked the girls what the stick game was and how they played it – the girls wouldn't tell her, just that they each played alone in a room with the adults. Elaine agreed with the sitter, that the stick game was huge cause for concern. It didn't sound good at all.

As soon as Doug got home from work, Elaine said they had to move. Things with Nancy's mother were getting out of hand and Jennie was becoming increasingly remote from the family and rebellious against their parental directives. She explained that Jennie had mentioned at least twice that Nancy's mother was a better parent because she didn't work. Doug was becoming outraged. He was upset about the comments as well but had no idea where to turn. They both believed that if there were activity in Nancy's house that was abusive to Jennie, they would have to be very careful. The members of Nancy's household may be engaging in criminal activity, which would endanger Jennie and the entire family. Elaine and Doug agreed that moving may be necessary at some point, but they would monitor the situation and see what they could do. They didn't want to uproot the family again so soon after building their dream home.

Doug remembered another girl in the neighbourhood, Jessica, had been going to Nancy's house as well. She was the same age as Jennie, four. He suggested they meet with Jessica's parents to inquire if they have had concerns too. Both agreed they would contact Jessica's parents; and they would have to approach the subject cautiously.

Jessica's parents, Jacob and Samantha, agreed to meet the next day. They seemed anxious to meet.

The meeting began at 8:30 p.m. the following evening. Both sets of parents wanted to meet after the girls were in bed. Both families had older children that could babysit while they met. They met at Doug and

Elaine's house in the family room with the French doors closed to keep their conversation private.

"So, Jacob and Samantha," Doug began, "we are quite concerned about what might be going on at Nancy's house. Jennie has had behaviours that have become a bit upsetting to us. Is this something you might have experienced with Jessica as well? Or are we giving you new information?".

Both Jacob and Samantha looked at each other quietly and did not seem to be surprised. They admitted that their daughter, Jessica, was acting very strangely as well. They were becoming increasingly concerned but had wondered if it was their parenting. They, too, had experienced the phrase "Show me your privates". They expressed relief that Doug and Elaine had approached them to meet.

Elaine and Doug told them that their concerns began about four months previous. Jennie had become difficult, loyal to Nancy's mother, was having health issues, and using language not consistent with her age level. Jacob and Samantha said they had had the same types of issues in their home with Jessica. Vaginal and urinary infections – doctors said were normal at their age. They said Jessica was becoming very quiet to an alarming level. She rarely talked to the family. She seemed to be robotic in behaviour, did what she was told without emotion, and seemed to hate school. She had always liked school.

All parents agreed that the police should be involved. They were very apprehensive about the prospect, but they knew they couldn't approach Nancy's family about it. Having to act secretively made them afraid. Elaine and Doug said they would call the police and see what the next step should be.

All of the parents were in an anxious state of disbelief. No parent wants to think their child has been abused by anyone, and certainly not by neighbours. Their daughters all played together and would be at Nancy's house for no more than two hours at a time.

All agreed that play time at Nancy's house must be terminated immediately. They knew their daughters would be upset, but there was no other choice. They hoped the police would act quickly before Nancy's family became aware.

In order to not make it too obvious, Nancy was permitted to come to their houses and play, under strict supervision by parents and sitters. All agreed this was the solution and to make sure the people in 'that' house were not alerted to any suspicions.

Elaine called the police the next day. She was extremely emotional, and a meeting was arranged at the police station for that afternoon. The officers were concerned and asked if they could meet with the parents immediately.

When Elaine arrived, she was asked to sit in the waiting room for the next detective. It seemed as though it took hours, but was only fifteen minutes. A female officer came out of the main office area and escorted her to an interview room. When Elaine told her what had been happening, the officer was quite cool and unemotional. She told Elaine she would have to interview Jennie. Elaine was reluctant and said she would call her husband to make sure it was okay.

Both parents agreed the interview should take place. Jennie may not say anything, but it needed to be done. When Elaine told Jennie, she said she would be talking to a really nice lady.

Elaine called her sister, Beth, to tell her about what was going on with Jennie and the neighbours. It was very difficult to share. Beth was shocked and very protective of Elaine, Jennie, and the whole family. She told Elaine she would do whatever the family needed. She felt close to Jennie, and would be happy to be there to help in any way. There always seemed to be a bond between Beth and Jennie. They were alike in many ways.

Jennie said she wanted Beth to be there when she spoke with the officer. Jennie knew Beth was coming for a visit. The police confirmed that having Beth in the meeting might be of benefit to Jennie.

When Beth arrived, she learned more details of what the two families were going through and was horrified. All of the little girls were only four years of age. Beth had experienced teaching children who had been sexually abused. She always consulted school student records in such cases, even though not all information was accessible by teaching staff. She found the situation with Jennie and Jessica disgusting and heartbreaking. She knew from her own experience; the girls would face a challenging future.

"Of course, I will go in with Jennie. I am honoured she wants me there and that you and Doug will support it." Beth kept her emotions in check out of respect for Elaine and Doug. She really had a bad feeling about it. She had noticed a change in Jennie as well, even in the short time she had been there for her visit.

The day arrived to go into the police station for the interview. Elaine, Beth, and Jennie were the only ones to attend. Too many people would have caused more concern for Jennie. Elaine and Beth gave each other their usual "I'm nervous" look and entered the room.

The minute they entered the interview room, Jennie jumped up on Beth's lap, which just warmed her heart. Beth gave her a big hug, and then the detective entered the room. She asked Jennie questions about her friend, Nancy, and what they did when she was visiting. Jennie said nothing that would indicate wrongdoing on the part of Nancy's family. She talked about their play times and never once indicated there was anything done that would be wrong. Discussion about the stick never became a part of the conversation.

Beth thought there should have been more questions asked. For example, do you have any secrets with Nancy or her mother? Do you ever feel uncomfortable in Nancy's house? Where do you play? Who is there when you are playing? She thought the detective was untrained regarding child interviews.

After the interview, the police explained that the initial interview questions should not lead a child for responses. The officer has to build a "trust" with the child. They said there is a process involved. Beth and Elaine then understood the reasons for the approach of the officer. They appreciated help from the police even more.

The one thing that Jennie said that shocked Elaine was when Jennie mentioned being in a hidden room. The officer did not ask her to explain the room further to make sure she did not lead the child. Jennie said that there were lots of people in the room and movies. She said that Nancy's mother used to watch movies in the room. Elaine had never heard about the room. Jennie was so non-communicative with the family, that Elaine wasn't surprised.

The interview lasted about 45 minutes. Elaine and Beth thanked the detective for her time. She told them she would be in touch soon.

Both women were exhausted after the interview. It was heartbreaking to see little Jennie having to go through all of this. They talked about the room that was hidden. Elaine told Beth she had never heard of it. Beth was even more concerned but reserved comment. She could see that her sister was extremely upset.

The next day, Elaine received a call from the police detective. The detective assured Elaine that children rarely speak of such events because predators instill fear very early in the grooming of children. She assured Elaine that action would be taken. Elaine asked her about the hidden room in the house. The detective said she had taken notes and it would be a consideration in the investigation.

Elaine called Beth with the news. Beth was very pleased and hoped it would happen very soon. She asked Elaine to keep her posted.

The family believed the investigation would begin immediately. They hoped it would because Nancy's family would become more aware of the situation because Jennie was no longer permitted to go to Nancy's house for playtime. Jennie was becoming even more agitated and difficult because of it all.

Elaine and Doug began discussing moving. After the police interview, they were very concerned that there might be retaliation from Nancy's family if they were suspicious. Nancy's mother, father, grandfather, and some uncles were living in the house or visiting on a regular basis. Elaine and Doug were warned by the police that if Nancy's family knew about the police investigation, they might have a threatening situation. The move would have to be done for the safety of the entire family and to remove Jennie from the source of the abuse.

Unfortunately, the police took four months to get the search warrant, which isn't unusual. They found computer and movies under a stairwell behind a false wall. So, there was a hidden room. Crimes in which digital devices are used were fairly new in the mid 1990's. The FBI started recording and studying the crime of digital child pornography in 1993, because the digital product of child pornography was just becoming known. When Beth was Network

Administrator during the 1990's, computers and devices were simpler than today. Child Pornography existed, computer and devices were used to produce and distribute it, but not with the degree of ease in today's digital world. At the turn of the century, animated gifs were just being introduced to the Internet. Pictures were being transferred by email. Secret websites for child pornography predators increased, but the knowledge of them by the general public was fairly limited. This crime is far more prevalent with today's technology.

The officers said they would have difficulty investigating all of the evidence because of staffing and time constraints. This type of response would never be tolerated in the maturing digital world of today because the crime is better known. All videos would be reviewed. Computers and digital devices have increased the ease with which predators can communicate. Technology has made it economical and easier for predators to access the pictures. At any one time on the Internet, it is estimated there are approximately three quarters of a million predators searching for child pornography. In Canada, it is illegal to search for child pornography.

The disappointment of the families about the lack of investigation was indescribable. A few years later, they learned from Jennie that both girls had been threatened: their daddies would be shot, their families would be hurt, they would be hurt, and the list went on. Not only was Nancy's mother involved, but the father, grandfather, and others were too. The girls spoke of a hidden room where they "played". The "postman" would always deliver packages to the home and pick up packages. The packages always contained movies. They never did find out who the postman was, but they suspected he was a delivery person for the videos, probably another family member.

There was no other place for the two families to turn. They had to pick up the pieces and forge on with their lives. Both families moved from the subdivision, their dream homes. They had to remove themselves from the environment of trauma. The girls might then have a fighting chance to survive without further damage.

Elaine and Doug moved to another area within the city. Their new home was in an area that was familiar with the family and one they could trust. They were always accepted in the neighbourhood. Jessica's family moved to another city. They kept in touch for a while and Jessica's family came back to let the girls play together sometimes.

Jennie eventually followed the path of so many sexually abused children. She fell in with the wrong crowd with drinking, drugs, and late-night parties. It was a difficult time for her parents. She was even more defiant and becoming a bit violent.

Elaine and Doug had to decide to have her put in a group home because of the effect on the family and her three siblings. The night she was admitted to the group home, she left. When the group home called, Elaine and Doug were absolutely distraught. The staff explained that youth who go into the home are not in a jail, and are free to leave if they want to do so. Doug went out to the streets to find her which was a very dangerous undertaking. Jennie's friends were street wise and sometimes, spent nights on the streets together. Jennie even slept on a park bench to stay with her friends and party.

After she left the group home, Jennie had gone to visit her sister, Judy, not far from where they lived and told her she would be going to a city close to their home for a little while. Judy called Elaine and Doug to tell them what Jennie had said. They were beside themselves. Elaine went to the city and drove around all of the streets where she thought she could find her daughter. It was a futile exercise, but Elaine thought she could not stay home and just wait for word. She had to do something.

When Beth found out about it, she told Elaine to forget about the city she was searching – she believed Jennie would be heading to a different province. Elaine didn't want to believe Beth. Beth put flyers up in the Salvation Army home for street people in the city in Ontario where she lived, and asked them to please call if they found her. The staff gave permission to post the flyer, but said quite often runaways stay away from facilities like the Salvation Army for fear of being caught. They know that would be the first place the police and parents would go to find a juvenile.

Within a week, Jennie was located. She and her friends had stolen a car from a friend's mother. Jennie had stolen a plate from her sister's car and put it on the stolen car thinking it would be harder to detect. She had, in fact, gone to Ontario Canada with her friends on an adventure. In later years, she told Beth she had gone to her home city. Beth had a premonition that was the case but could not find her.

Jennie and her friends had been busking to get money for food and sleeping in the car. They washed their hair in Wal-Mart washrooms. The family heaved a huge sigh of relief when she was found. They then had to deal with the results of her actions after she had run away from the group home. Luckily, she was a minor and adult charges were not laid.

Jennie had many emotional challenges as a teenager, resulting from her abuse by the neighbours when she was a child and started living a life style that was not familiar with the family. Nothing made her feel better or helped her get rid of the memories.

She began living with different people. After a while, she started living with a boyfriend. He tried to kill her by beating her. He wouldn't let her out of their apartment. A neighbour called the police. Elaine and Doug were called and flew to the apartment as fast as they could. When they arrived, Jennie was in a fetal position in the back seat of the police car, protecting her badly bruised face and body. The boyfriend had beaten her so badly her parents didn't recognize her. She had to live with Elaine and Doug for a while because of the danger she was in at the apartment. They eventually removed all of her belongings and Jennie moved into another apartment, alone.

Jennie had quit school at the age of 16. After a few years, she decided to complete her education. She had a determination that was becoming a positive energy experience rather than the negative energy she had lived in earlier years. Jennie seemed to become more responsible, which made her parents, grandparents, aunts, uncles, and siblings very proud. She attended a college where she took administrative studies resulting in her being qualified as a Veterinary Assistant.

At the age of 18, she had a baby. She was very careful with her diet during her pregnancy. She was so excited to be pregnant that she wanted to tell everyone. Jennie gave birth to a healthy baby boy, "Ben". Elaine and Doug, for many reasons, had to take Ben in because Jennie was having difficulties with her relationships and the responsibilities of caring for a baby.

Eventually, Jennie had Ben over to her apartment for weekends. He always looked forward to seeing his mother. They would pitch a tent in the living room and camp in the apartment. Jennie and Ben would go swimming at the pool or lake, go walking in the local park and have quality time together. These visits were gradual and if Jennie's boyfriend was over, Ben was only permitted to stay one night. The boyfriend wasn't always good with Ben.

Jennie managed to find an apartment that had two separate bedrooms. It was reasonably priced and in a good location of the city. Her mother helped her move in. It was exciting because Elaine was going to rent an apartment down the street so that Ben and Jennie could see each other more often. Ben would have his own room. This was a first step to Jennie having Ben full time. Both were becoming quite happy about it.

The first week they were there, a new friend who had helped her move in, came to the apartment and asked her if she would like to go out for some beers and party. She was ecstatic and Elaine took Ben home with her. She thought Jennie would benefit from a night out with friends. As always, Jennie had been lonely, and this seemed to be a night that she could see people and have a good time. Jennie said "I love you Mum." Elaine responded with "I love you too, sweetheart." Elaine and Ben left and Jennie got ready to go out.

Elaine talked to her sister to tell her she was so happy. She said Jennie has friends, a new apartment for her and Ben, and nothing could be better. They were all happy at this prospect.

At 5:30 a.m. the next day, July 15, 2012, Elaine was in her kitchen and the police came knocking at her door. They told her Jennie had been in a car accident and "did not make it". The driver was drunk. One other passenger in the car did not make it either.

Elaine fell back into a wall. She was alone with Ben and could not believe what she was hearing.

The fear she and Doug had all of these years had come true – Jennie had been killed. They wondered at times if it would be murder, suicide, or drug overdose but never thought of a drunk-driving incident. Elaine could not stop crying.

Elaine called Doug, who was working out of town. She called her son, Steve, to see if he could come to her house to help her out. She called her daughter, Judy, and son, Noah. She called her mother. And then....

Elaine called Beth at 6:19 a.m. and told her the terrible news. Beth screamed and began crying immediately. The devastation was indescribable. She could only think of poor Jennie and then cried out "Poor Ben!". She yelled out to her husband, "Mike, Jennie was killed in a car accident. Oh my God!". She called her son and told him. He was in total shock.

Beth and her husband got into their car within two hours and drove to Elaine's to help support the family and attend the funeral. Beth was hysterical, and drove most of the way home crying. She insisted on driving because it kept her mind occupied. Mike kept navigating and they managed to get there within 1.5 days, about 1,200 km.

Jennie was a victim of two major crimes – child pornography and drunk driving. Beth kept thinking about it. What a horrible time for the entire family, from the grandparents to her parents and siblings. She was so worried about Ben.

How can so many dark situations happen to one family? The loss was incredible. Beth's and Elaine's sister had been lost to cancer and the same sister's son died in a plane crash just two years before she died. Cancer death, plane crash death, child pornography victims, drunk driving death.

The funeral for Jennie was so quiet and emotional. Everyone was in shock. Ben was only four and did not understand the meaning of death. He did not attend the funeral. It took Elaine and Doug at least four years to explain that he would never see his mother again.

Many people attended. They had the funeral at a downtown church to ensure all of Jennie's friends could attend. The church was just about full. It warmed all of their hearts to have so many in attendance. Even the Lieutenant Governor of the province attended.

Newscasters covered the accident across Canada. It was so sad.

The burial followed the funeral. It was a beautiful, sunny day. Doug went over the Beth and asked if she liked the site. She said it was perfect for Jennie. It overlooked the huge river.

Elaine, Doug, and Beth stood together at the burial, arms wrapped around each other. Beth was overwhelmed with grief and could not believe the strength of Elaine and Doug. They played one of Jennie's songs from the stereo of the car. During the playing of the song, a butterfly kept fluttering over their heads until it finished. Maybe it was the spirit of Jennie.

Elaine and Doug worked to adopt Ben, officially. It went through and all members of the family were relieved. They have never regretted this. He is the joy and apple of their eyes. His eyes are identical to Jennie's, which is both difficult but comforting to them. Elaine and Doug, their children, Beth and all members of the family will never be the same after such a tragic end to a very troubled life. Jennie had only four years of innocence in her young life. What a travesty.

Eventually, the drunk driver was charged with two counts of drunk driving causing death, one count of drunk driving causing bodily harm. For the trial, Beth called Elaine and told her she would return home to support Elaine and Doug. The entire family sat in a row in the court room.

At one point, Doug went over to Beth after a court staff member spoke to him and Elaine. He said "they are going to be showing pictures of Jennie in the car.

It is up to you if you want to stay". Beth asked Doug if they were staying. Doug said "yes". Beth decided to stay and endure the showing of the pictures.

They showed Jennie in the car and other pictures. It was so sad for all of them. The driver was interviewed and did not seem to have remorse at all.

Result? He was sentenced to serve two, five-year sentences, to be served concurrently. He served them in the local prison in the beginning. Because so many of Jennie's friends were in the same prison, he had to be moved to another prison in another province because of assaults. He is now out of prison.

So many people think he should have done more time. There are no winners in this situation. Four friends out to party for a night. The irresponsibility of the driver to drive drunk on alcohol and cannabis. Jennie and the other passenger will never be back......

CHAPTER 26

MY STORY

I am "Beth" in the true story about Jennie. It has been very challenging for the entire family. Her death was in 2012. We are still in disbelief that it happened. Her mother, my sister, has had a very difficult time ever since. The look in her eyes will never be the same.

I, too, have had negative experiences involving sexual assault, but at ages 15 and 21, much older than the age of four when Jennie was sexually abused. I have first-hand knowledge regarding how much these types of traumas can affect someone for the rest of their life. Trust becomes a great issue. I can identify with sexual assault victims because of my experiences. Readers will come to realize that these true stories have a tremendous negative impact on the lives of the victims and their families.

One of the worst incidents in my life occurred when my high school teacher sexually assaulted me. I was on a school trip with a teacher and another student, Betty. We were there with a club from the high school, and were in discussions about international issues involving youth. There were students from across Canada.

Betty and I were billeted in different homes. It was nice because the billet families could speak French – both homes had only French-speaking families. The supervising teachers stayed in a hotel in the French City. The hotel sits on the sea and has a beautiful architecture and view.

After three days of being billeted, Betty and I decided we wanted an adventure and decided to put our money together and stay at the hotel. Our teacher supervisor was there and we thought we would be safe.

We called the hotel and were able to obtain a two-bed room at a reasonable price. We apologized to our billeting families and went to the hotel. I was pleased because my host family drove me to the hotel. I felt as though I had insulted them, but the adventure was just too great to pass up. The hotel was magnificent.

We told our teacher, Mr. Stu Pid (Mr. S) we were going to be staying at the hotel. Mr. S. was about 40 years of age, dark hair, glasses, slightly balding, and fairly trim. He stood about 6 foot 2 inches tall. He was very pleased we would be staying at his hotel, asked for our room number, and said he would stop by later to check on us. We felt safe because our teacher was being attentive. The adventure seemed to be going very well.

Later, I heard a knock at the door. When I opened it, Mr. S. was standing in the doorway with his arm leaning on the door frame. He said I should never open the door to anyone unless I know who it is.

I was alone. Betty had gone shopping with another friend. I was wearing my favourite blue jeans and a red shirt. Mr. S. sat down on the bed and asked me to sit beside him. He started to hold my hand and began to talk to me. His hand began to move up my arm and to my chest. I became very uncomfortable. I was a very innocent and naïve 15-year-old.

I asked myself, what is he doing? Where is this leading? He said "let's get silly on the bed and have some fun!". I immediately removed his hand and just looked at him and said "What do you mean by silly?" He grabbed my hand again and hugged me, "Oh, just silly, you know. You are the nicest and prettiest young girl I know." I responded with "No, I don't know. Please take your hand away...now." I pulled his hand away and pushed him off me. Mr. S. responded with, "You know, maybe we should leave the room and go somewhere. I can hardly help myself." I was quite happy to leave the room. I was shaking and sick to my stomach.

He took my hand and asked me to go on the fire escape. I went with him. He was very tall and dominant. I thought at least we were out of the bedroom. He put his arms around me and gave me a kiss on the lips as he was massaging my chest. I was disgusted and completely repulsed. His breath reeked and the whole situation was unnerving. I pushed him away and he grabbed me again. I pushed him and told him to stop and left the fire escape. I was crying inconsolably.

He followed me and turned me by my shoulder. Through tears, I told him he needed help and to leave me alone. He looked, and told me to keep it "our secret". He didn't want to lose his job, his wife, and his family.

It was a terrible experience. I saw him a number of years later in a restaurant when I was visiting my family. My mother was with me. I asked my mother if it was Mr. S. She looked over and said she thought he was. All of a sudden, our eyes met, and he kept staring. He at least turned purple. I glared at him and then looked away. I have a number of teachers in my family. It will never be something I will ever understand. How could anyone be in a position of authority and take advantage of it?

For many years, I have blamed myself for this experience. Did I act with too much enthusiasm when I was around him? Did I smile too often or make him think I was actually interested in him? Could I have avoided it?

These are all questions I now know I can answer. IT WAS NOT MY FAULT. After a few years of therapy, my therapist asked me what I would say to a victim of similar assault. I said, without hesitation, that it was not their fault. With that statement, I realized I was just a baby at the time. At the age of 15, Mr. S. took advantage of his dominant position and my naivety. It has taken years to come to this realization. And.... I still can relapse into wondering but with maturity, realize, it was his fault, not mine.

Four years later I was attending university. I was in a lab, alone, completing an assignment. It was 6:30 p.m. in January. There was a snow storm outside. I thought I should leave soon but needed to complete the assignment. It was dark and walking in a snow storm would not be a good plan.

My professor, Prof. Pred Ator (Prof. P.), came into the lab. I could smell beer on his breath and his hair was a mess. He came over to asked what I was doing. I explained I was finishing the assignment he had given and due the next day.

He came closer to me, which made me feel uncomfortable. I started feeling the same way I did in high school. I started to get extremely angry, to the point of my hands shaking. He pulled up my shirt, touched my breast, and tried to kiss me. This time, I pushed him so hard, told him to get away, and went running out of the lab. I used so much force, it equalled the two sexual assaults together.

I ran home crying. I couldn't believe it happened again. My run down the hill was with energy I didn't know I had. This time, I wasn't going to let another pervert off with it. He claimed to be a good religious man, but his behaviour illustrated otherwise.

I told my family about it. The professor was known to be a "good, religious" man. I spoke to my Sociology professor about it. He encouraged me to discuss it with some of the authorities at the university. I did. Unfortunately, I was treated as though I was a liar. I was embarrassed, outraged, and full of tremendous anxiety because of it. Now, I can understand why so many women are full of anxiety if they report it. At least the "me too" movement has helped women to be more open and less afraid.

Did anything come of it? Of course not. He was kept on at the university. I was made to feel terrible because of the entire incident. However, ten years later, I had great satisfaction. The professor had a number of complaints recorded against him, and he was removed from the staff of the university.

These kinds of experiences destroy the victim's trust in other people. To have this type of assault occur twice has made me suspicious of people in positions of authority. My experiences in life helped me to understand Jennie so well. To be assaulted at such a young age, was terrible. Poor Jennie.

I was a secondary school educator until I experienced a road-rage accident. The injuries caused permanent damage in my neck and back. I also have brain damage causing challenges with numbers – if I have a headache or am fatigued, I cannot compute easily. I had to resign from teaching because of it.

My specialty in education is Computer Science, with network management. I have held many positions using this expertise. In one part-time contract position, I was fixing and reimaging computers. "Reimaging" involves formatting the hard drive of a computer and installing a new operating system on the machine – no previous user files will exist on a hard drive after formatting and reimaging. I reviewed the machines, repaired, and reimaged them daily for distribution.

When reviewing one machine, I decided to do a jpg search (picture files). I had a supporting technician with me. I performed the search because I had a suspicion there may have been files on the machine that shouldn't have been there. When we looked at the screen, all of a sudden child pornography came up. Pictures of children aged from about four to eleven in sexually explicit positions. We both froze. The effect of seeing such pictures was indescribable.

I have had flashbacks of these pictures every day. The poor little girls. One picture looked so much like Jennie that I am sure she was. It gave me an unwelcomed realization of what she went through. How can anyone do such vile acts with a child and why? Disgusting.

I became very upset because of the pictures. Trying to cope with the flashbacks became very painful. I found my emotions very difficult and left my work post many times with uncontrollable crying. I made an appointment with my physicians. "Dr. O" was very sympathetic and told me that I needed to leave the workplace for a while. I took a week of sick leave and hoped it would help.

My doctor gave a diagnosis of PTSD. I had to ask her what it meant. She explained it was Post Traumatic Stress Disorder. After the diagnosis, I started realizing the PTSD acronym was being used all the time, connected to many traumatic incidents in society, not just war experiences. I began to understand that the results of seeing the pictures, having so many flashbacks, and being woken in the night from nightmares were all related to PTSD.

I believed that no one could ever understand why I felt so terrible. One can try to overcome abuse, but eventually, the feelings of worthlessness, despair, and horror surface and take over. My experiences with the teacher and professor, along with Jennie's horrendous experience, also contributed to my feelings of hopelessness and despair. I began to realize my trust of people was so much less. My reactions to some situations was far more dramatic than ever before. I attended some sessions that helped me understand my reactions and why they were occurring. I am sure some of my friends were scratching their heads, wondering what had happened to me.

My advice to anyone who has received the PTSD diagnosis is to shop for a therapist who will help. Make sure it is someone they trust and the gender that is the most compatible to them and to their needs. My choice ended up being a female therapist. She gave me the support I needed and allowed me to be myself in all sessions. She would explain emotions, why, and how I could cope better with the challenges.

I will always be grateful to "J.F.". Her quiet, patient personality gave me more strength than I am sure she realizes. She stated at one session, I had changed so much. She remembered my strained, pale face the first few months but that I gradually became more relaxed, trusting, and full of vitality. I went from an emotional wreck, to being a global speaker, sharing my Theory of Digital Supervision in different countries. Could I have done that years before? Not on your life. Gratitude cannot even explain my feelings of her devotion and true interest in what I was doing. If I am in crisis, she sees me and picks up where we left off. She never forgets.

It has given me the incentive to have a determination I would not have had otherwise. Thank you "J.F.".

CHAPTER 27

STARTING THE CHARITY

I sat down at my computer one day in tears, with the realization Elaine would never be the same again, nor would my entire family. Every time I talked to Elaine or looked at her, it broke my heart, and still does. She laughs and jokes as she always has, but there is such an indicator of tremendous grief and hurt always.

When she talks about Jennie, she is emotional and says she will never get over her death. My response has always been "I know you never will. Who could.". People I have known who have lost a child are the same way. It is a black hole in their heart that will never be mended.

I thought "what can I do to help Elaine and the entire family?" I started doing searches on google and tried to get some ideas. Jennie had been a victim of child pornography and drunk driving. I am a Computer Specialist and Network Administrator in education. Could I do something?

It came to me – maybe begin a charity that would be in memory of Jennie? I spoke to my mother and she said what about all of the other children who are victims? I decided to begin a charity in memory of Jennie and in support of all victims. We would have fundraising for therapy for victims of child pornography.

I had no idea where to begin and decided to contact a lawyer who specializes in charity law. We met. She told me it could cost anywhere from $8,000 to $25,000 to start the charity but advised if I was interested in proceeding, to use the education approach. I told her I was interested in educating the public about the dangers of the Internet and the necessity of child protection online. She agreed it would be a good idea and said she would like to assist in any way she could.

Knowing she would be expecting the huge bill to be paid, I knew it wouldn't happen. I did not have the money nor did I have any idea how to obtain it.

I decided to do my own research and see if I could begin the charity without legal assistance. I called the Canadian Charities Directorate and they advised as long as all paper work is complete, a lawyer may not be necessary.

After my call to them, I sat down and went through their website, printed out all forms that were required, and proceeded to plan out my strategy to begin my charity. I used a service in Toronto to coordinate the papers, at a much lesser cost than a lawyer. The day after the conviction of the drunk driver who killed Jennie, I submitted my papers wondering if I was doing the right thing. It cost $1,200 but I was willing to do it. I crossed my fingers and hoped for the best.

That was in April 2014. In May, 2014, we became a not-for-profit corporation with the name "Child Pornography Hurts" (name changed to "Internet Sense First" January 2018) and had our first Board of Directors meeting. I had asked people to be directors whom I believed would be good for the charity.

My next quest was to become a registered charity so that we could issue income tax receipts, a requirement of Canada Taxation to be able to issue receipts. I planned the submission, talked to senior officials at Canada Charities Directorate, and we became a registered charity January 1, 2015, apparently in record time.

I will never forget my joy when we received our corporate seal. It was worth the countless hours at the computer and on the phone to so many people. At my first Board of Directors meeting, I used the seal. My first Board members were very good people. Two are still with the Board and loyal to the cause. Others had to leave for different reasons. We have 15 consultants that assist in our day-to-day operations. At the writing of this book, all members of the organization are volunteers. We believe all monies raised should go to the children, whether in therapy or through education sessions.

Not long after the start-up of Child Pornography Hurts, the Board of Directors developed a Twitter account, to be used as an informative medium to the public. In November 2014, the board member who managed it called me and stated he had received a child pornography picture. I was horrified. He asked what he should do.

We notified the Internet Child Protection unit of the local police who went to the board member to get a statement. The police determined that the tweet originated in a city in the United States. Within one week, I received a copy of an email from Homeland Security of the United States informing me that a nineteen-year-old predator had been arrested and the infant had been rescued. Yes, the victim was an infant. People ask me how old children are to be victimized and I tell them "0 to 18 years".

In 2018, Board members proposed that the name be changed. They submitted that sometimes people will go around our banner and signs, hoping their children would not see it. I found this strange because the words "child pornography" are all over the news, both print and TV/radio. They are not foreign to children. In fact, when I speak at schools, if I ask children of any age what they think "inappropriate pictures" are, they respond immediately with "child pornography".

However, I did find when I was trying to get people to come to events, when I stated the charity name, they sometimes just stopped the conversation. This type of attitude is one that predators love. People who do this are only supporting their crime of "secrets" – secrets with our most vulnerable sector, our children. I asked Board members to think of a new name.

After two meetings, we decided on the name "Internet Sense First – Premier Sens Internet". We have the term "Internet Sense" with registered copyright. It can be defined to mean common sense regarding safety on the Internet. Internet Sense First only made "sense". It was done and is now our official name. I had to admit to Board members, answering the phone when in a group setting with the new name was easier. If I answered Child Pornography Hurts, people would always look over with their eyebrows raised!

I searched for a unique logo for the new name. I did not want to have a computer, mouse, or anything else that could be duplicated. The flower "white heather" is supposed to be a protection flower, used by Scottish warriors when they went into battle. It was perfect. The Board of Directors voted "yes" to the new logo. Our logo is round, the beautiful picture of white heather in the middle, reference as "White Heather The Flower of Protection".

My journey continues daily. The issue of children being victimized online is a global issue. My love and compassion for children should be unquestioned.

It is my goal to have the term "Digital Supervision" used as a common term in households, schools, communities, working with youth – everywhere. Our children need us more than ever before in the history of the world. They are the most independent than they have ever been – we need to realize it and pull them back from the cyber world consuming them. Parents, grandparents, professionals – we are up to the challenge and we can do this – we must.

CHAPTER 28

CONCLUDING STATEMENTS

The Internet and social media can have many positive channels. Families can feel more connected, particularly if they live a distance away from each other. With the Internet, we have many luxuries. Information and data are just a keyboard away. It is safe to say we use the Internet daily, whether directly or indirectly.

We cannot be bystanders any longer. Adults need to choose to adopt Digital Supervision and apply it regularly so that children and youth in their care will be in a better position to make better choices. In addition, it is important to avoid giving children full ownership of their choices online. *Ownership of the guidance, protection, and supervision of children is still the responsibility of adults.*

To summarize recommendations:

Communicate with children daily about their online activities.

Realize when children are online gaming, they are on another server and require supervision. Play online games with your children, either in person or anonymously to learn how and with whom they are communicating. Study the gaming system and know it thoroughly.

Install a hardware filter and realize it must be considered interdependent with Digital Supervision.

Install a keylogger on devices to record all keystrokes and activity. It should be a keylogger that does not record passwords. Malware can capture passwords recorded with keyloggers (and in other environments as well).

Mirror the cellphone of your children to monitor their activities. Install a keylogger or filter.

As much as possible, have emails originated and written by children forwarded or copied to parents/caregivers for monitoring. Realize, they will eventually have emails unknown to parents/caregivers.

Check all browsers on devices to ensure there are no dark web browsers (providing anonymity – IP addresses are hidden).

Review all pictures and web histories on all devices periodically. As much as possible, instill in children that only a parent can erase histories. Although difficult to monitor, it will give the message to children/youth the device is provided by you and will be monitored for their protection.

Review any software environments to ensure that webcams, facetime, Skype, or similar apps are not being used to create inappropriate videos. Check all video files on all devices periodically.

Review Skype, FaceTime, Twitter activity and possible Periscope use, and/or other similar apps. Ensure there is no real-time transmission. New apps are being created all the time. Real-time transmission is the favourite of predators.

Turn off the router or unplug the network cable on your router at night. Keep your router in the parental bedroom if possible. Take the necessary actions to protect against electrical waves with the router in the parental bedroom.

Check for unsecure wireless routers in your area. Alert any neighbours within wireless access if their router is not secure to avoid children accessing such a router.

Check geolocators on all devices. This feature can alert an unknown as to the location of the device to a predator.

Exercise caution when emailing unknowns and educate children about the dangers. The header on the email can reveal location and more details about the origin of the email.

Know your child's passwords on all devices and monitor/review the devices regularly. Try to avoid giving the router password to your child. If they obtain a burner cellphone, they will be able to access the Internet through your router.

Teach your children that humanity must still exist and this should be respected as much online as it is in person. Humanity in this context would be the entire human race or the characteristics that belong uniquely to human beings, such as kindness, love empathy, mercy and sympathy.

Communicate with children/youth regularly regarding safety, predation, sharing of personal information, gaming with knowns only, and more. Communicate without villainizing children for being victims of a digital world that is consuming this generation.

Above all, please love and hug your children frequently. They need compassion and guidance in a computer driven world that can create a lack of sensitivity to humanity. Please remember to apply Digital Supervision.

APPENDIX A

COMMON ACRONYMS FOR (S)TEXTING

When practicing Digital Supervision, parents, grandparents, and adult allies must be familiar with common acronyms used for texting. When using a keylogger, it is important to understand the abbreviations. The following list gives multiple acronyms but not all. It is a good introduction to texting to facilitate application of Digital Supervision.

Symbols used:

!	I have a comment
:<>	Amazed
:-X	Big kiss
%-)	Confused
☹	Crying

:e	Disappointed
☺	Disgusted
o-&-<	Doing nothing
:*)	Drunken smiling face
O-S-<	In a hurry
:-*	Kiss
:-D	Laughing
:o	Ooooh! Shocked
☹	Sad
:-@	Screaming
☺)	Very Happy
;-)	Winking
121	One to one
143	I love you
14AA41	One for all and all for one
2BZ4UQT	Too busy for you Cutey
2G2B4G	Too good to be forgotten
2G2BT	Too good to be true
2moro	Tomorrow
2nite	Tonight

2U2	To you too
404	Haven't got a clue
411	Information
420	Marijuana
459	I love you
4COL	For crying out loud
4EAE	For ever and ever
4NR	Foreigner
53X	Sex
831	I love you
86	Out of, over, to get rid of, or kicked out
9	Parent is watching
911	Emergency – call me
99	Parent is no longer watching

Acronyms and Phrases:

A/S/L/P	Age/sex/location/picture
A3	Anyplace, anywhere, anytime
AAYF	As always, your friend
ADR	Address

AFC	Away from computer
AITR	Adult in the room
AML	All my love
ASL	Age/sex/location
AYFT	Are you free tonight?
AYSOS	Are you stupid or something?
BB4N	Bye bye for now
BBIAW	Be back in a bit, few, sec, while
BF	Boyfriend or best friend
BFF	Best friends for ever
BIF	Back in five
BRB	Be right back
BRT	Be right there
BR	Bathroom
BTCOOM	Beats the crap out of me
BTOIYB	Be there or its your butt
BTW	By the way
C-P	Sleepy
CD9	Code 9 – parents are around
CIL	Check in later

CRB	Come right back
CS	Career suicide
CT	Can't talk
CTC	Care to chat
CUL8R	See you later
CYE	Check your email
CYL	See you later
CYT	See you tomorrow
DAK	Dead at keyboard
DEGT	Don't even go there
DF	Dear friend
DGT	Don't go there
DIAF	Die in a fire
DIKU	Do I know you
DLTM	Don't lie to me
DOC	Drug of choice
DTRT	Do the right thing
DTTMN	Don't talk to me now
DURS	Darn you are sexy
DWB	Don't write back

DWPKOTL	Deep wet passionate kiss on the lips
DYHAB	Do you have a boyfriend
DYHAG	Do you have a girlfriend
E123	Easy as one, two three
EG	Evil grin
EL	Evil laugh
EMA	Email address
EML	Email me later
F2F	Face to face
F2T	Free to talk
FAWC	For anyone who cares
FF	Friends for ever
FIL	Father in law
FOC	Free of charge
FTF	Face to face
FWB	Friends with benefits
FYEO	For your eyes only
G4I	Go for it
G4N	Good for nothing

GA	Go ahead
GBH	Great big hug
GFN	Gone for now
GGN	Gotta go now
GGOH	Gotta get out of here
GL	Good luck or get lost
GNBLFY	Got nothing but love for you
GNSD	Good night, sweet dreams
GTG	Got to go
GTGP	Got to go pee
H&K	Hugs and kisses
h/o	Hold on
H4U	Hot for you
H8	Hate
HAK	Hugs and kisses
HAY	How are you
HB	Hurry back
HHIS	Hanging head in shame
HIG	How's it going
HOIC	Hold on I'm coming

IAE	In any event
IAYM	I am your master
ICYC	In case you are curious
IDC	I don't care
IHY	I hate you
ILY	I love you
IME	In my experience
IMRU	I am. Are you?
IMS	I am sorry
IWALU	I will always love you
J/C	Just checking
J/J	Just joking
J/K	Just kidding
J/P	Just playing
J/W	Just wondering
JDI	Just do it
JT	Just teasing
K, KK, OK	All mean okay
KFY	Kiss for you
KHYF	Know how you feel

KK	Kiss Kiss
KOTC	Kiss on the cheek
KOTL	Kiss on the lips
KPC	Keeping parents clueless
KYPO	Keep you pants on
L8R	Later
LDL	Let's discuss live
LDR	Long distance relationship
LFTI	Looking forward to it
LJBF	Let's just be friends
LKITR	Little kids in the room
LLC	Lady looking cool
LMIRL	Let's meet in real life
LMK	Let me know
LMTCB	Left message to call back
LOML	Love of my life
LONH	Lights on nobody home
LY	Love you
LY4E	Love you forever
LYB	Love you babe

LYL	Love you lots
M2NY	Me too not yet
M4C	Meet for coffee
M8	Mate
MB	Message board
MHBFOR	My heart bleeds for you
MIRL	Meet in real life
MITIN	More information than I need
MLAS	My lips are sealed
MLF	My love forever
MLOS	Mom looking over shoulder
MorF	Male or female
MOS	Mom over shoulder
MSG	Message
MUSM	Miss you so much
NAB	Not a blonde
NAPC	Name address postal code
NLL	Nice little lady
NME	Enemy
OLL	Online love

OOC	Out of control
OOI	Out of interest
OST	On second thought
P	Partner
P&C	Private and confidential
P911	Parent alert
PA	Parent alert
PAL	Parents are listening
PAW	Parents are watching
PBB	Parent behind back
PBEM	Play by email
PCM	Please call me
PDA	Public display of attention
PDS	Please don't send
PFM	Please forgive me
PIR	Parent in room
PLOS	Parents looking over shoulder
PO	Peed off
POMS	Parent over my shoulder
POS	Parent over shoulder

PRW	Parents are watching
PTMM	Please tell me more
QT	Cutie
RL	Real life
RLCO	Real life conference
RLF	Real life friend
RMLB	Read my lips baby
RN	Right now
RT	Real time
RU/16	Are you over 16?
RU/18	Are you over 18?
RUKM	Are you kidding me?
RUMORF	Are you male or female?
S2U	Same to you
SB	Stand by
SCNR	Sorry could not resist
SED	Said enough darling
SETE	Smiling ear to ear
SHMILY	See how much I love you
SIT	Stay in touch

SITD	Still in the dark
SLAP	Sounds like a plan
SLF	Sounds life fun
SMEM	Send me email
SMIM	Send me instant message
SOZ	Sorry
SSC	Super sexy cute
STTM	Stop talking to me
STYS	Speak to you soon
SU	Shut up
SUP	What's up?
TAS	Taking a shower
TAW	Teachers are watching
TCFW	Too cute for words
TCS	Take care sweetheart
TDTML	Talk dirty to me later
TIAIL	Think I am in love
TNT	Til next time
TOA	Text on arrival
TOM	Tomorrow

TTUL	Talk to you later
TTYT	Talk to you tomorrow
U	You
U2	You too
UNTCO	You need to chill out
UOK	Are you ok?
UPOD	Under promise over deliver
UR	You are
UTM	You tell me
VBG	Very big grin
VBS	Very big smile
VM	Voice mail
VSF	Very sad face
W8	Wait
W84M	Wait For Me
WAFS	Warm and fuzzies
WAK	What a kiss
WAY	What are you doing?
WAY	Where are you?
WAYD	What are you doing?

WB	Welcome back
WBS	Write back soon
WC	Who cares
WCA	Who cares anyway
WFM	Works for me
WILCO	Will comply
WRUD	What are you doing?
WTGP	Want to go private?
WTH	What the heck?
WTM	Want to meet?
WYCM	Will you call me?
WYRN	What's your real name?
WYS	Whatever you say
WYSIWYG	What you see is what you get
X-I-10	Exciting
XLNT	Excellent
XOXO	Hugs and kisses
YBS	You'll be sorry
YBY	Yeah baby yeah
YDKM	You don't know me

YIWGP	Yes I will go private
YM	Your mother
YNK	You never know
YOYO	You're on your own
YTB	You're the best
YT	You there?
ZZZ	Sleeping, bored, tired
^5	High five

APPENDIX B

DEFINITIONS

It is important for parents and adult allies to understand terminology related to computer use and applications. Knowledge is power. As part of Digital Supervision, knowing words, terms and definitions brings more understanding. With more understanding, comes more effective Digital Supervision.

Bandwidth –describes the speed at which data travels within connectivity. The greater the bandwidth, the faster data will be sent, gaming can take place, and other Internet activities. Different environments require more bandwidth, and if the bandwidth is low, the speed of the environment being used is slow.

CPU Cache – used by the computer to provide speed of access to data. It is a smaller memory which stores data from main memory locations, and is frequently used. There can be multiple levels of CPU caches.

DNS – Domain name system – This is a system used to convert alphabetic names into numeric IP addresses. For example, when a website is entered (example: www.internet.com), the DNS converts the URL into the IP address (example: 204.0.8.52). The DNS allows users to enter names of websites rather than the IP address. Very few people would remember numbers as opposed to names, which provides ease of use.

FaceTime – Begun by Apple in 2010, this is used on iPads and iPhones. Users will contact someone through their iPad or iPhone and be able to engage in one-on-one video chats. This is problematic when children and youth decide to transmit nudes to the recipient user. Laptops, with webcams, are used for this purpose as well, but simply referred to as webcam video.

Filter – email services use filters to separate regular email from spam. Everyone should be aware of this definition because email is so common. There can be another type of filter used to separate desirable websites from undesirable ones. This type of filter helps to keep younger children out of inappropriate websites. A new type of filter actually provides a "Bright Web" so that the Internet is actually separated for child use. Once in place, the child will only be able to access the Bright Web. This type of filter is a piece of hardware, interfaced between the router and the computer.

Free Private Chat Rooms – Users can sign up for private chats with one or more people. Children or teens in this type of environment should be monitored as to the people in the chats.

Free Video Chat rooms – Users can have webcam videos exchanged through these rooms. Obviously, these types of chats need to be monitored through Digital Supervision application.

Hackers – It is illegal to hack into a computer network, yet children and youth believe it to be "funny". They often try to do it just to prove they can. Parents need to discuss this type of activity with their children and explain the possible legal actions that can be taken against them if they do this. Activity can be traced. Ground rules should be made with children by the parent/caregiver to ensure that the child/youth does not put themselves in any type of compromising situation with law enforcement.

Host – A computer or network connected to the Internet.

Internet Protocol Address – Often referred to as the "IP" address. This is a unique number that is different for each computer. "Unique" should be interpreted the same way as a cell phone or phone number. Phone numbers are unique worldwide, as are IP addresses.

Modem or Router – Device for connecting a host to the Internet. Routers and modems used to be separate but are now usually combined into one unit.

Online Sexual Exploitation – Victims can have a predator make demands for money. A victim could have exposed themselves and knowingly or unknowingly been recorded by a predator. They may threaten the victim that the pictures or videos will be shared with other friends on Facebook or other social media. Unfortunately, sometimes the recording was done without the knowledge of the victim. A well-known victim of this type of sextortion was Amanda Todd.

OS – The operating system of a computer, cellphone or other digital device. The OS manages the computer hardware and input devices such as mouse, keyboard, headphones, and more. The OS helps all of the parts and software work together. It should be viewed as the same as an engine on a car.

Peer-to-peer networking – A network in which file sharing can be done without easy detection. This is commonly referred to as P2P activity. If computers are connected on a P2P basis, all connections must have a common file-sharing program in order to connect (Torrent, KaZaa, Morpheus, Limewire, and more)

Phishing – The act of attempting to obtain personal data from users. This is usually done through the use of email. People receive an email with a subject line such as your account with a company is past due. You are then asked for personal information such as financial. A person's credit card number, social insurance number, and other information could be requested. Therefore, it is referred to as "phishing" because the hacker is "fishing" for information.

Public Chat Rooms – Forums where people can chat about a number of topics. For example, politics, sports, education, and the like.

Remote Access Tool (RAT) – allows an attacker to gain full control of a user's computer when installed. Microsoft Windows-based computers are the most susceptible to this malware.

Revenge Porn – Children and youth use this to exercise revenge against another child or youth. If they have pictures that can be humiliating or embarrassing, they will use the pictures in an act of vindictiveness such as a boyfriend's former girlfriend or a girlfriend who has turned into someone's enemy. Adults can engage in this type of activity as well.

Screen Capture – Copying what is currently displayed on a screen to a file or printer.

Search Engine – not to be confused with web browser. A search engine is used to acquire data. More common search engines are google, yahoo, and others.

Self-exploitation – Children and youth creating, sending, possessing or sharing videos/pictures using webcams, cell phones, iPads, messaging applications or other electronic cellular devices. To be self-exploited, these pictures would be of a personal nature.

Selfie – Using an electronic device (particularly cell phones) of people taking pictures of themselves.

Server – A computer configured to provide a service to enable communication between computers and/or devices in a network, including access to software and central storage of files. When online gaming, gamers will operate from a server for the specific game they are playing.

Sexting – Users use cell phones to text sexual comments or to send nudes of themselves to other users.

Theory of Digital Supervision – A three-part theory.

- Awareness – what is truly happening on the Internet and what vulnerabilities do children have while using digital devices;
- Method – how can adults, guardians, and adult allies supervise children effectively;
- Hope – we can do this and we must. The basis of the Theory is parents, grandparents, adult allies have a responsibility to children through

supervision of their online activities. This is a combination of open communication, sharing of information with children that is necessary for them to make the right choices, and technological methods to supervise children while on devices.

URL – Universal Resource Locator – A web page's unique location or address. The reason it is referred to as "universal" is because web page will appear the same in any browser or computer operating system.

User – any human being using a computer, cell phone, digital device.

Viewing Pornography – it is illegal for anyone to sell hardcore pornography to anyone under the age of 18 in Canada. Yet, it is free online.

Web browser – a program required to "surf" the world wide web, or more commonly called the Internet. There are various types of browsers, for example, Internet Explorer, Safari, Chrome, and more.

APPENDIX C

THE CANADIAN CRIMINAL CODE

DEFINITION OF CHILD PORNOGRAPHY

For accuracy, this section is taken directly from the Canadian government website:

https://laws-lois.justice.gc.ca/eng/acts/c-46/section-163.1.html

- **163.1(1)** In this section, ***child pornography*** means
  - **(a)** a photographic, film, video or other visual representation, whether or not it was made by electronic or mechanical means,
    - **(i)** that shows a person who is or is depicted as being under the age of eighteen years and is engaged in or is depicted as engaged in explicit sexual activity, or

- - **(ii)** the dominant characteristic of which is the depiction, for a sexual purpose, of a sexual organ or the anal region of a person under the age of eighteen years;
  - **(b)** any written material, visual representation or audio recording that advocates or counsels sexual activity with a person under the age of eighteen years that would be an offence under this Act;
  - **(c)** any written material whose dominant characteristic is the description, for a sexual purpose, of sexual activity with a person under the age of eighteen years that would be an offence under this Act; or
  - **(d)** any audio recording that has as its dominant characteristic the description, presentation or representation, for a sexual purpose, of sexual activity with a person under the age of eighteen years that would be an offence under this Act.
- **Marginal note:Making child pornography**
  (2) Every person who makes, prints, publishes or possesses for the purpose of publication any child pornography is guilty of an indictable offence and liable to imprisonment for a term of not more than 14 years and to a minimum

punishment of imprisonment for a term of one year.

- **Marginal note:Distribution, etc. of child pornography**

  (3) Every person who transmits, makes available, distributes, sells, advertises, imports, exports or possesses for the purpose of transmission, making available, distribution, sale, advertising or exportation any child pornography is guilty of an indictable offence and liable to imprisonment for a term of not more than 14 years and to a minimum punishment of imprisonment for a term of one year.

- **Marginal note:Possession of child pornography**

  (4) Every person who possesses any child pornography is guilty of

  - **(a)** an indictable offence and is liable to imprisonment for a term of not more than 10 years and to a minimum punishment of imprisonment for a term of one year; or

  - **(b)** an offence punishable on summary conviction and is liable to imprisonment for a term of not more than two years less a day and to a minimum punishment of imprisonment for a term of six months.

- **Marginal note:Accessing child pornography**

  (4.1) Every person who accesses any child pornography is guilty of

  - **(a)** an indictable offence and is liable to imprisonment for a term of not more than 10 years and to a minimum punishment of imprisonment for a term of one year; or

  - **(b)** an offence punishable on summary conviction and is liable to imprisonment for a term of not more than two years less a day and to a minimum punishment of imprisonment for a term of six months.

- **Marginal note:Interpretation**

  (4.2) For the purposes of subsection (4.1), a person accesses child pornography who knowingly causes child pornography to be viewed by, or transmitted to, himself or herself.

- **Marginal note:Aggravating factor**

  (4.3) If a person is convicted of an offence under this section, the court that imposes the sentence shall consider as an aggravating factor the fact that the person committed the offence with intent to make a profit.

- **Marginal note:Defence**

  (5) It is not a defence to a charge under subsection (2) in respect of a visual representation that the accused believed that a person shown in the representation that is alleged to constitute child pornography was or was depicted as being eighteen years of age or more unless the accused took all reasonable steps to ascertain the age of that person and took all reasonable steps to ensure that, where the person was eighteen years of age or more, the representation did not depict that person as being under the age of eighteen years.

- **Marginal note:Defence**

  (6) No person shall be convicted of an offence under this section if the act that is alleged to constitute the offence

  - **(a)** has a legitimate purpose related to the administration of justice or to science, medicine, education or art; and
  - **(b)** does not pose an undue risk of harm to persons under the age of eighteen years.

- **Marginal note:Question of law**

  (7) For greater certainty, for the purposes of this section, it is a question of law whether any written material, visual representation or audio recording advocates or counsels sexual activity with a person under the age of eighteen years that would be an offence under this Act. 12

FOOTNOTES

1 "Pornography Addiction." - Wikipedia, the Free Encyclopedia. Wikimedia Foundation. Web. 12 Apr. 2016.

2 "Definition of Addiction". American Society of Addiction Medicine Public Policy Statement. August 15, 2011.

3 "Pornography Addiction Statistics", August 21, 2019. Retrieved from: https://keyloggers.mobi/pornography-addiction-statistics/.

4 Researched Statistics. Updated 2019. Retrieved from: https://www.thorn.org

5 "Sextortion". Wikipedia the Free Encyclopedia. Web. Last updated September 20, 2019.

6 "Police-reported Sexual Offences against Children and Youth in Canada, 2012." Government of Canada, Statistics Canada., 2014. Web. Jan.-Feb. 2016.

7 Plake, Sarah. "KSHB 41: Children abusing children, Children's Mercy sees' dangerous trend involving

children and pornography". Kansas City. Dec. 5, 2018.

8 "Child-On-Child Sexual Assaults Soar, Police Reveal". 2017. Retrieved from: https://www. theguardian.com/society/2017/oct/09/child-on-child-sexual-assaults-soar-police-figures-reveal

9 Dr. R. Dyson, Paper for CPRA Conference, University of British Columbia, Congress of the Social Sciences and Humanities, June 5 - 7, 2019.

10 "11 Facts About Cyberbullying". 2019. Retrieved from: https://www.dosomething.org/us/facts/11-facts-about-cyber-bullying

11 Thomson Reuters. "Teen Sexting May Be More Common Than You Think". Feb. 26, 2018. Retrieved from: https://www.cbc.ca/news/health/sexting-teen-1.4552532

12 Canadian Criminal Code. "Definition of child pornography". Amended June 17, 2019. Retrieved from: https://laws-lois.justice.gc.ca/eng/acts/c-46/section-163.1.html.

CITATIONS

"Age of Consent to Sexual Activity." Government of Canada, Department of Justice, Electronic Communications. Web. 5 Nov. 2015.

"An Act Respecting the Mandatory Reporting of Internet Child Pornography by Persons Who Provide an Internet Service (S.C. 2011, C. 4)." Legislative Services Branch.

"Humanity Dictionary Definition | Humanity Defined." Your Dictionary. Web. 1 May 2016.

"Operation Avalanche (child Pornography Investigation)". Wikipedia. Wikimedia Foundation. Web. 7 Apr. 2016.

"Metadata". Wikipedia. Lasted edited August 23, 2019. Retrieved from: https://en.wikipedia.org/wiki/Metadata

"Online Tech Dictionary for IT Professionals." Webopedia. 2019. Retrieved from: https://www.webopedia.com

"Photo DNA". Wikipedia. Last edited May 28, 2019. Retrieved from: https://en.wikipedia.org/wiki/PhotoDNA

"What is an IP address. "What is an email header?". (Copyright 2019). Retrieved from: https://whatismyipaddress.com/email-header

Admin. "Erectile Dysfunction Increases among Young Men, Sex Therapist Brandy Engler, PhD." Your Brain On Porn. 25 July 2013, 22:12. Web. 17 Mar. 2016, 10:30 a.m.

Andrews, Caron C. "Protecting Children from Pornography Addiction: A Therapist's Advice". (Copyright 2019). Retrieved from: https://educateempowerkids.org/protecting-children-pornography-addiction-therapists-advice-2/

Beck, Jacob. "How Pornography Effects Teenagers (and children)". Copyright 2017. Ever Accountable.

Brantford, News. "Teen Charged with Distributing Intimate Image." Brantford Expositor, News Brantford, Brant, 21 Jan. 2016. Web. 25 Jan. 2016.

Canadian Criminal Code. "Definition of child pornography". Amended June 17, 2019. Retrieved from: https://laws-lois.justice.gc.ca/eng/acts/c-46/section-163.1.html.

Carey, Tanith. "Why More and More Women Are Using Pornography." The Guardian. Guardian News and Media, 07 Apr. 2011, 21:00,. Web. Apr. 2016.

Carn, Billie. "The Internet of Humanity [IoH]." The Huffington Post. TheHuffingtonPost.com, 4 May 2016, 3:24 p.m. ET. Web. 8 May 2016, 8:00 p.m.

Cooper, Roy. "Is Your Child At Risk Online?" Is Your Child At Risk Online? North Carolina Department of Justice. Web. 5 Feb. 2016.

Dr. R. Dyson, Paper for CPRA Conference, University of British Columbia, Congress of the Social Sciences and Humanities, June 5 - 7, 2019.

Educate and Empower Kids, "How To Talk To Your Kids About Pornography", Rising Parent Media, 2018.

FBI. "Overview and History of the Violent Crimes Against Children Program." FBI. FBI, 2010. Web. Jan.-Feb. 2016.

Finch, Samantha. "Online Sexual Predators Baiting Children Caught in Police Sting." Parent Herald RSS. Parent Herald, 10 Apr. 2016, 6:20 p.m. Web. 12 Apr. 2016.

Fowler, Sarah. "You don't realize you're being manipulated: Child predators often groom parents first". April 23, 2019.

Government of Canada, 23 Mar. 2011. Web. 4 Jan. 2016.

Haas, Elson M., MD, "Staying Healthy With Nutrition", Ten Speed Press, 2006.

Harper, Elizabeth. "What is Facebook Account Cloning & What Can You do about It?". March 7, 2019.

Hendrickson, Megan. "What Is Malware? Here's What You Need to Know to Keep Your Website Safe", June 7, 2018.

Hinduja, Sameer Ph.D., Patchin, Justin W. Ph.D. "Cyberbullying: Identification, Prevention, and Response". 2019 Edition.

Internet Society. "Brief History of the Internet". Published 1997. Retrieved from: https://www.internetsociety.org/internet/history

Kelly, Amanda, "10 Laval Teens Face Child Pornography Charges; Girls Unaware Photos Shared". Global News Toronto,, 14 Nov. 2014. Web. 5 Mar. 2016.

King, Miriam. "Think, before You Hit Send." Bradford Times. Bradford Times.ca, 20 Mar. 2014., 4:28 EDT p.m, Web. Feb.-Mar. 2016.

Krueger, Richard B. "The Impact of Internet Pornography Use and Cybersexual Behavior on Child Custody and Visitation". 4 April 2013.

Lewis, Marieke, Patrick Miller, and Alice R. Buchalter. "Internet Crimes Against Children: An Annotated Bibliography of Major Studies." Loc.Gov. Federal Research Division, Library of Congress, Washington, D.C., Oct. 2009. Web. Feb.-Mar. 2016.

Lieberman, Caryn, and Adam Miller. "Toronto Woman's Webcam Hacked While Watching Netflix." Global News Toronto Womans Webcam Hacked While Watching Netflix. Global News Toronto, 10 Aug. 2015, 11:07 a.m. Web. 22 Jan. 2016.

M'Jid, Najat Maalia. "Child Pornography Flourishes in a World with No Borders." United Nations Human Rights, Office of the High Commissioner, 29 Nov. 2009. Web. 2 May 2016.

McRoberts, Meghan. "Sexting Acronyms Parents Need to Know." WPTV. 10 Dec. 2014. Web. 12 Mar. 2016.

Meissner, Dirk. "Sexting B.C. Teen Found Guilty of Child Pornography." British Columbia. The Canadian Press, 10 Jan. 2014. Web. 21 Feb. 2016.

Mesmer, Aaron. "Sheriff, School Take on Lake Placid Teen Sexting Scandal." WTVT. Fox 13, 18 Feb. 2016, 6:41 p.m. Web. 21 Feb. 2016, 11:15 a.m.

Mick, Jason. "Unsecured Routers Land People in a Heap of Police Trouble -." Daily Tech. Daily Tech, 15 Apr. 2011. Web. 5 Jan. 2016.

Moran, Lee. "North Carolina Teens Arrested for Sending Nude Selfies, Videos to One Another: Cops." New York Daily News. 21 Sept. 2015. Web. 5 Mar. 2016.

National Society For the Prevention of Cruelty to Children "Grooming". (copyright 2019) Retrieved from: https://www.nspcc.org.uk/preventing-abuse/child-abuse-and-neglect/grooming/

Ncmec. "The Real Story: Victim of Sexual Abuse Speaks out." Missing Kids. NCMEC, 2014. Web. Mar. 2016.

News, CBC. "Teens Charged with Distributing Child Porn Online in Kamloops - British Columbia - CBC News." CBCnews. CBC/Radio Canada, 13 Feb. 2014. Web. 2 Jan. 2016.

Olson, Heidi. "Sexual Assault Expert Warns of Heartbreaking Trend Among Children". Copyright 2019. Glen Cove Press.

Pulido, Ph.D. Mary L. "Child Pornography: Basic Facts About a Horrific Crime." The Huffington Post. TheHuffingtonPost.com, 17 Oct. 2013, 12:54 p.m. Web. Jan.-Feb. 2016.

Pulido, Ph.D. Mary L. "Exploring Why Offenders View Internet Child Pornography." The Huffington Post. TheHuffingtonPost.com, 29 Feb. 2016. Web. Mar.-Apr. 2016.

Pulido, Ph.D. Mary L. "Fighting Internet Child Pornography." The Huffington Post.

Race, Sharla. "The truth about BHA, BHT, and TBHQ and other antioxidants used as food additives". 2009.

Ryan, Patty. "A Victim of Child Pornography Doesn't Get to Forget." Tampa Bay Times.13 Dec. 2013, 1:08 p.m., Web. 12 Feb. 2016, 12:15 p.m.

Sherwell, Philip. "US Investigators Arrest 14 'operators' of Massive Global Child Pornography Website." The Telegraph. Telegraph Media Group, 19 Mar. 2014. Web. Jan.-Feb. 2016.

Tech Terms "Filter". (Copyright 2019 Sharpened Productions). Retrieved from: https://techterms.com/definition/filter

The Bark Team. "What is Grooming? The signs to look for with sexual predators". July 19, 2017.

The Conversation. "One in seven teens are sexting". Retrieved from: https://theconversation.com/one-in-seven-teens-are-sexting-says-new-research-92170

TheHuffingtonPost.com, 19 July 2014. Web. Jan.-Feb. 2016.

WBUR. "Snapchat 'Has Become A Haven' For Child Predators, Criminal Justice Scholar Says". January 2018. Retrieved from: https://www.wbur.org/hereandnow/2018/01/22/snapchat-child-predators

Wikipedia "Child Grooming". (last edited September 7, 2019). Retrieved from: https://en.wikipedia.org/wiki/Child_grooming

Wikipedia. "Sextortion". Last edited September 10, 2019. Retrieved from: https://en.wikipedia.org/wiki/Sextortion

Winters, Georgia M. and Jeglic, Elizabeth. "Stages of Sexual Grooming: Recognizing Potentially Predatory Behaviors of Child Molesters". 2018 Taylor and Francis Group. March 2016.

Wright, Michael P. "Ensis Wiki." - Pedophilia in Ancient Greece and Rome. Ensis Wiki. Web. 21 Mar. 2016.

Refuse to be a bystander
Choose to protect
Choose to apply Digital Supervision.

In the words of Benjamin Franklin "Justice will not be served until those who are unaffected are as outraged as those who are." Be proactive.

CPSIA information can be obtained
at www.ICGtesting.com
Printed in the USA
LVHW091339151019
634201LV00001B/5/P